CICERO: SELECT LETTERS

A Companion to the Translation by L.P. Wilkinson

CICERO
SELECT LETTERS

A Companion to the Translation
by L.P. Wilkinson
with Introduction & Commentary by

M.M. Willcock
Professor of Latin, University College London

Published by Bristol Classical Press
General Editor: John H. Betts

Cover illustration: Cicero, from a portrait bust, Vatican
Museums, Rome [drawing by Jean Bees]

Printed in Great Britain
ISBN 0−86292−195−3
Published (1986)
by
Bristol Classical Press
Department of Classics
University of Bristol
Wills Memorial Building
Queens Road
BRISTOL BS8 1RJ

Willcock, M.M.
    Cicero: select letters: a companion to the
translation by L.P. Wilkinson.
    1. Cicero, Marcus Tullius — Criticism and
interpretation
    I. Title   II. Wilkinson, L.P.
    876′.01   PA6320

ISBN 0−86292−195−3

Typeset by Florencetype Limited, Bristol
Printed in Great Britain by
Short Run Press Ltd, Exeter

Contents

Preface

This Commentary is a collection of explanatory notes on the translation of a selection of Cicero's Letters by Patrick Wilkinson (*Letters of Cicero*, Geoffrey Bles Ltd 1949, repr. Bristol Classical Press 1982). It has been a source of pleasure to compose, for I am indebted to Mr. Wilkinson for much kindness in past years. He died in 1985, before the publication of this commentary; but he knew of the undertaking and generously encouraged it.

To the books which he recommended for further study in 1949 (pp. 11–12), the following may be added:

Caesar, *Civil War*, Book I

Cambridge Ancient History, Vols. IX and X (Cambridge 1932 and 1934)

E. Rawson, *Cicero: A Portrait* (London 1975; repr. Bristol 1983)

D.R. Shackleton Bailey, *Cicero* (New York 1971)

D. Stockton, *Cicero: A Political Biography* (Oxford 1971)

R. Syme, *The Roman Revolution* (Oxford 1939; pbk 1960)

Mr R.A. England gave me permission to make use of notes which he himself had composed on this selection of Letters; Mr T.E.J. Wiedemann read the whole in typescript and made numerous helpful comments and suggestions; colleagues at University College London, Drs T.J. Cornell, N.M. Horsfall, J.A. North, and R.W. Sharples, answered particular questions and saved me from error; Mrs A.F. Bright-Holmes gave accurate help with the typescript. To all of these I express my thanks.

M.M. Willcock
August 1985

Note: Page and note references are to Wilkinson, not to this commentary. '*Introduction*', however, indicates the pages immediately following here; 'Wilkinson, *Introduction*' the other volume.

Introduction

1

53   Cn. Domitius Calvinus, M. Valerius Messalla Rufus
       Death of Crassus
52   Cn. Pompeius Magnus III, Q. Caecilius Metellus Pius
       Scipio
51   Servius Sulpicius Rufus, M. Claudius Marcellus
       Cicero goes to his proconsular province of Cilicia
50   L. Aemilius Paullus, C. Claudius C. f. Marcellus
49   C. Claudius M. f. Marcellus, L. Cornelius Lentulus
       Crus
       Caesar invades Italy
48   C. Julius Caesar II, P. Servilius Isauricus
       Battle of Pharsalus; Death of Pompey
47   Q. Fufius Calenus, P. Vatinius
46   C. Julius Caesar III, M. Aemilius Lepidus
45   C. Julius Caesar IV; Q. Fabius Maximus, C. Trebonius;
       C. Caninius Rebilus
44   C. Julius Caesar V, M. Antonius; P. Cornelius
       Dolabella
       Caesar is assassinated. Octavian appears on the scene
43   C. Vibius Pansa, A. Hirtius
       *The 'second triumvirate' is formed, of Antony, Octavian
       and Lepidus; proscription and death of Cicero*

II THE EXTANT CORRESPONDENCE OF CICERO

The Letters of Cicero, as they have been transmitted to the modern world, are divided into thirty-seven books:

1. The Letters to Atticus (*Ad Atticum*) in sixteen books contain 426 letters, dating from November 68 to November 44, in more or less chronological order. In contrast with the letters *Ad Fam.* (below), all the letters – apart from occasional enclosures which are usually official communications sent by Cicero for Atticus' information – are from Cicero to Atticus; there are none from Atticus in reply.

2. The Letters to his Friends (*Ad Familiares*) in sixteen books contain 435 letters, dating from January 62 to August 43. The letters are both from Cicero to his numerous correspondents and from them to him. The distribution into

sixteen books is complex: for the first twelve books, and Book XV, the letters are mostly in blocks, to (and in many cases from) the same correspondent and, within the block, in essentially chronological order; thus, for example, Book IX contains twenty-six letters, first eight to Varro, then six to and from Dolabella, then twelve to Paetus. Book XIII represents a particular genre, letters of recommendation by Cicero on behalf of friends to numerous people in authority, such as governors of provinces. Book XIV contains letters to his wife Terentia; Book XVI those to Tiro, Cicero's freedman and a close member of his family, who is the most likely person to have put together the collection after Cicero's death.

3. The Letters to his Brother Quintus (*Ad Quintum Fratrem*) in three books contain twenty-seven letters, dating from the year 60 to December 54. All the letters here are from Marcus to Quintus, none the other way (although we do have writings by Quintus, among the letters to Tiro in *Ad Fam.* XVI and a pamphlet about the handling of an election which Quintus apparently wrote for his brother in advance of the consular elections for 63).

4. The Letters to Marcus Brutus (*Ad Brutum*) in two books contain twenty-six letters, all from the last year of Cicero's life, between March and July 43. Here, as in *Ad Fam.*, the correspondence is two-way, letters both to and from Brutus.

There are very difficult questions about the origin and survival of this fascinating collection. Cicero's only reference to the possibility of publication is in a letter of 44 B.C. (**132** in this selection), where he speaks of Tiro having collected about seventy. Ancient sources mention other letters in addition to those that have survived.

Two complete editions facilitate study. R.Y. Tyrrell and L.C. Purser (T/P) of Trinity College, Dublin, edited the complete collection in chronological order in seven volumes between 1879 and 1901, with later editions of individual volumes up to 1933. Inevitably some of the information has been superseded by more recent scholarship, but this is a most useful work. More recently, D.R. Shackleton Bailey (SB), formerly of Jesus College, Cambridge, and now of Harvard University, has given us one of the finest achievements of modern scholarship: the *Letters to Atticus* appeared in seven volumes between 1965 and 1970, those *Ad Familiares* in two volumes in 1977, and those to Quintus and Brutus in a single volume in 1980, all published by the Cambridge University Press. The *Letters to Atticus* have a translation on the page facing the text; the others do not. SB's translations of all appeared in three volumes in the Penguin Classics series in 1978.

The present selection was made by L.P. Wilkinson of King's College, Cambridge, and first published in 1949. It contains 147 letters, many of them however only in part. The state of affairs is made clear by the reference at the end of each letter. *Ad Fam.* V, 7 (Letter **1**) means that the whole of the seventh letter of the fifth book of *Ad Familiares* is quoted; *Ad Fam.* V, 6, 2 (Letter **2**) means that only the second paragraph of that letter is given (it consists in fact of three paragraphs). Mr Wilkinson published his translation for the general reader; for that reason he chose to give the modern forms of many place names; and in some cases he exercised considerable ingenuity in finding a well-known modern quotation (e.g. from Milton or Thomas Gray) to give a similar effect to a literary (usually Greek) quotation by Cicero in his letter.

III THE END-DATE OF CAESAR'S SECOND PROCONSULAR COMMAND IN GAUL

It is an extraordinary fact that we do not possess clear evidence for a key date, that of the termination of the second five-year command in Gaul awarded to Caesar as a result of the 'Conference of Luca' in 56 B.C.; we do not even know that a precise date was laid down. It is clear that Caesar was concerned about what might happen when his command in Gaul came to an end, and for that reason asked to be allowed to stand for a second consulship in absence, before he ceased to be governor of Gaul. By the usual rule that there should be ten clear years between a person holding the same office, this ought to have been for the year 48 B.C., and he would thus have wished to stand in absence in an election in the summer of 49; but it is possible that he wished for dispensation from that rule too, and to stand in 50 for the consulship of 49. The plan to stand in absence was a way of avoiding a period as a private citizen, when he would be liable to prosecution for past illegalities.

A successor to the Gallic provinces might be appointed at any time; but the normal procedure, if a consular governor was to be sent, would be for the senate to decide in advance of the consular elections in the summer of a given year that Gaul would be one of the consular provinces. In that case one of the two consuls then elected would proceed to Gaul some eighteen months later.

From 52 onwards we hear of manoeuvres in the senate, by opponents and friends of Caesar (the latter mostly as tribunes, exercising their right of veto), to try to manipulate this situation. No doubt our present uncertainties reflect confusion existing at the time. If however we knew of a precise date when the five-year proconsular command was due to end, we could perhaps better understand the aims of these manoeuvres; and surely we should know for which year (49 or 48) Caesar originally wished to stand in absence. Different views have been held. The great historian Mommsen argued that Caesar's command ended on 1 March 49; others have supported 1 March 50, or 13 November 50 (so F.E. Adcock in *Cambridge Ancient History*, Vol. IX, p. 617). On the other hand, it may be that no precise date was fixed. The most important evidence is in Cicero's Letters; the problem is how to interpret it. Wilkinson's selection contains most of the significant statements, all except one being in letters from Caelius to Cicero:

30 (May 51) 'Marcellus has held up his proposal about the succession to the governorship of Gaul, postponing it to June 1.' Cf. **70** (a letter from Cicero to Atticus dated February 49, but referring to past events) 'Pompey opposed the consul Marcus Marcellus when he was for fixing March 1 as the closing date for Caesar's governorship of Hither and Further Gaul.'

37 (August 51) 'The senate has voted that Pompey should return to the capital as soon as possible, so that the matter of the assignment of provinces may be dealt with in his presence.'

42 (October 51) 'Pompey has said that it would be out of order for him to give a decision on Caesar's provinces before March 1, but that after that date he will have no hesitation.' (Later in the same letter) 'Caesar is willing to accept one of two alternatives: either to stay where he is, and not have his name put forward for the consulship this year, or, if he can first secure his election, to give up his province.'

53 (June 50) 'Pompey seems so far to have thrown his weight on the side of the senate, to the effect that Caesar should retire on November 13.'

54 (June 50) 'You will be glad to hear that our friend Curio's veto regarding the provinces had excellent results.'

58 (August 50) 'Whereas Pompey is determined not to allow Caesar to become consul unless he gives up his army and provinces, Caesar is convinced that he cannot be safe once he has parted with his army.'

It is easily seen from these excerpts why we do not know the answers to the problems. Caelius writes allusively, and of course both he and Cicero were fully familiar with the facts of the situation. The crisis progressively deepened, until on 11 January 49 Caesar crossed the Rubicon and invaded his own country.

The following Letters, or parts of Letters, are covered in this Companion. The number in the right hand column refers to the letter number in the Commentary, and to the number in the Bristol Classical Press edition of Wilkinson's *Letters of Cicero*. Note that this number is absent from all earlier editions.

Ad Att.			*Ad Att.*		
I	13.3-4	**3**	VII	7.5-7	**63**
I	16.3-5	**4**	VII	17.3-4	**66**
I	18.1-3; 6-7	**5**	VII	20	**67**
II	1.4-8	**6**	VIII	1	**69**
II	3.2-4	**7**	VIII	3.1-6	**70**
II	6	**8**	VIII	9.1-3	**76**
II	18	**9**	VIII	9.4	**71**
II	19.2-5	**10**	VIII	11B.1; 3-4	**68**
III	7.1	**11**	VIII	13	**72**
IV	1.4-8	**13**	IX	6.1; 3-4	**73**
IV	3.2-3; 5	**14**	IX	16	**74**
IV	4A	**16**	IX	18.1; 3	**75**
IV	5	**17**	IX	19.1-2	**77**
IV	6.1-2; 4	**19**	X	18.1-2	**79**
IV	10	**22**	XI	6.2-5	**81**
V	1.1; 3-5	**29**	XI	18	**82**
V	10.1-3; 5	**31**	XI	23.3	**84**
V	12.1	**34**	XI	24.2-3	**85**
V	13.1	**35**	XI	25.3	**83**
V	14.1	**36**	XII	2	**88**
V	15	**38**	XII	4	**90**
V	16	**39**	XII	12	**101**
V	21.10-13	**46**	XII	18.1	**99**
VI	1.5-8; 21	**47**	XII	19.1	**100**
VI	2.4-5	**49**	XII	32.2-3	**102**
VI	3.1-2	**52**	XII	35	**104**
VI	6.1	**56**	XII	36	**105**
VII	1.2-7	**60**	XII	40.1	**106**
VII	4	**62**	XIII	12.1-3	**109**

Commentary

1 *To Pompey, in Asia Minor*   *Rome, Summer, 62 B.C.*

p.32   **My great zeal on your behalf**: In 66 Cicero supported the proposal by the tribune Gaius Manilius that Pompey be given the command against Mithridates (in the extant speech *Pro Lege Manilia*); he also, as consul in 63, proposed an official Thanksgiving at Rome for Pompey's success, and probably did the same again in 62, on the receipt of the 'official despatch' mentioned earlier in this letter.

    Scipio ... Laelius: P. Cornelius Scipio Aemilianus (Africanus Minor) was the leading general and politician at Rome in the middle of the second century B.C., much admired by Cicero; he was the centre of the 'Scipionic Circle', a group of intellectual and civilised friends interested in bringing Greek culture to Rome. Of these the closest to Scipio was C. Laelius, consul in 140 B.C. They were famous as friends as well as like-minded public men. Cicero has Laelius speak of Scipio in his work *De Amicitia* (*On Friendship*), and uses them, as well as other members of the Circle, as the interlocutors in his dialogue *On the Republic* (see **27**).

2 *To Sestius, in Macedonia*   *Rome, December, 62 B.C.*

Publius Sestius was a supporter of Cicero in his consulship, and later in the disorders of the early 50's. In 56 Cicero successfully defended him against a charge of assault, in the speech *Pro Sestio*. At this time Sestius was quaestor in the province of Macedonia, with the proconsul M. Antonius, who had been Cicero's consular colleague in 63.

    A house: on the Palatine hill.

    3500 sestertia: i.e. 3,500,000 sesterces.

The man who rescued the bankers: Catiline, like other revolutionaries, had proposed the abolition of debts.

3 *To Atticus, in N.W. Greece*   *Rome, January 25, 61 B.C.*

p.33   **The Good Goddess**: *Bona Dea.* A sacrifice was made to her on behalf of the people of Rome at the beginning of December, at a night ceremony from which men were excluded. The event described here caused a massive scandal at Rome.

A man in woman's clothes: Publius Clodius, son of Appius Claudius Pulcher, consul in 79, and a member of one of the most ancient Roman families. He affected the plebeian form of the family name, Clodius rather than Claudius.

Cornificius: Q. Cornificius had been praetor in 67 or 66.

The Right: *boni viri*, 'sound citizens of substance and conservative views' (SB on *Ad Att.* I 12.1).

Draconian: Cicero says 'Lycurgan', from the Spartan law-giver. Draconian is a more familiar reference in English, from Draco, the severe Athenian law-giver of the seventh century.

4 *To Atticus, in N.W. Greece*   *Rome, June, 61 B.C.*

p.34   **Blames Hortensius**: It is explained earlier in this letter that Hortensius (consul in 69, and the leading orator at Rome until the ascendancy of Cicero) had supported a proposal for the random selection of the jury for this trial, instead of their appointment by the praetor, on the grounds that he did not believe any jury could acquit Clodius.

Senators ... knights ... treasury officials (*tribuni aerarii*): These were, since 70 B.C., the three classes from which a jury was selected, in equal proportion from each of the three (Wilkinson, *Introduction*, p. 28).

Xenocrates: an Athenian philosopher, follower of Plato. 'Your fellow-Athenians' is a friendly joke based on Atticus' name.

Metellus Numidicus: consul in 109, Rome's general against Jugurtha; his honesty and independence are often praised by Cicero.

Tell me now: *Iliad* 16.112−3, the turning point of the *Iliad*, when Hector finally managed to set fire to one of the Greek ships.

My trumpet-blower: cf. Wilkinson, *Introduction*, p. 22.

5 *To Atticus, in N.W. Greece*   *Rome, January 20, 60 B.C.*

p.35   **Camillus (?)**: The transmitted reading is Metellus, who would have to be Q. Metellus Celer, consul this year, husband of the notorious Clodia (p. 38, n. 2). Most modern commentators think it incredible that Cicero should have been even on potentially friendly terms with this old-fashioned aristocrat. Thus Shackleton Bailey hesitantly suggested the similar name Camillus, a private friend of Cicero (cf. **93**). But Metellus was now a neighbour on the Palatine, and Cicero does speak later in this paragraph of his 'spectacular friendships with the great', so that perhaps the scepticism of commentators is unwarranted.

p.36   **Sands and shores**: from an unknown Latin poet.

A consul thrust upon us: L. Afranius, described in *Ad Att.* I 19.4 as a total nonentity. He was later Pompey's commander in Spain (**65**).

A motion about bribery and about juries: This is explained in another letter (*Ad Att.* I 17.8), which mentions 'the promulgation under a senatorial decree of a bill providing for an investigation into the conduct of jurors guilty of taking bribes' (trans. SB). The Knights vociferously objected. The matter is referred to again in Letter **6**, p. 39.

p.37   **Their precious fishponds**: This is a repeated criticism of the extreme optimates on the Senate, that they were more interested in their luxurious lives than in the good of the state; cf. p. 39.

Reception of foreign delegations: This took place in February each year.

The letter is *Ad Att.* II 1 (not I 1 as in the text).

Tribune of the plebeians: see p. 38 n. 1.

It was an inheritance he was seeking: presumably by getting himself adopted (as he was in the following year, by a plebeian called P. Fonteius; cf. **63**). If Clodius said this, he said it as a joke.

p.38   **Patricians like him**: the Catilinarian conspirators.

My protégés: Cicero had upheld the cause of the Sicilians in his prosecution of Verres in 70.

She wages: The words form a iambic line of verse, and are thought to be a quotation from an unknown comedy.

Fabius: unknown.

The Land Bill: This was a proposal by a tribune called Flavius to make land available for Pompey's veterans from the East (referred to in more detail in *Ad Att.* I 19.4). The history of Land Bills (*leges agrariae*) goes back to Tiberius Gracchus in 133; they were a repeated source of conflict between 'popular' tribunes and the Senate.

p.39   **A consul thrown into prison**: Metellus, by the tribune Flavius, for blocking his Land Bill.

Bribe these men: i.e. the Knights.

7 *To Atticus, on his way home*   *In the country, ? December, 60 B.C.*

p.40   **I must resist the Land Bill**: This is a new one, the first of two to be brought forward by Caesar in his consulship of 59, aimed primarily at providing land for Pompey's veterans.

Solonium: between Rome and Ostia; Cicero must have had a villa there, as he did at Anzio.

Cornelius Balbus: a very able Spaniard, now a Roman citizen, who plays a large rôle in the next twenty years; see Index.

Book III of my poem: This was a poem in epic hexameters which Cicero wrote on his consulship; little survives.

The motto of Hector: *Iliad* XII 243.

Compitalia: a festival held on January 1st.

Pomponia: Atticus' sister, married to Cicero's brother Quintus.

Theophrastus: Aristotle's successor as head of the Peripatetic school of philosophy.

8 *To Atticus, at Rome*   *Anzio, April, 59 B.C.*

Eratosthenes: an Alexandrian polymath, who wrote on geography among other subjects; Serapion and Hipparchus were other scholars in this field. Tyrannio was a Greek who lived at Rome, gave instruction in Cicero's house (see Index), and later taught the most famous geographer of ancient times, Strabo.

Butrinto: Buthrotum, on the west coast of Greece, now Albania. Atticus preferred to live there.

Vatinius: P. Vatinius, now tribune and a supporter of Caesar, a coarse and ugly man, much disliked by Cicero.

Theopompus: a fourth century Greek historian, of severe moral tone.

The Left: i.e. the radical and unreliable citizens; see note on 'The Right', **3**.

9 *To Atticus, on his way to N.W. Greece*   *Rome, Summer,*
                                          59 B.C.

Curio: C. Scribonius Curio, a very able and personable young man of good family, seemed at this time to be a focus of opposition to the triumvirs, although he later became a strong supporter of Caesar; see Index.

Fufius: Q. Fufius was praetor in this year, and another supporter of Caesar. He and Vatinius became consuls in 47.

The Campanian Land Bill: the second and more extensive of the two bills promoted by Caesar.

Laterensis: M. Juventius Laterensis, a distinguished and honourable politician (Syme, *The Roman Revolution*, p. 179), who achieved the praetorship in 51.

Caesar has most handsomely: Caesar offered Cicero the post of legate in his forthcoming proconsular province of

Gaul, just as he had already offered him a place among the twenty land commissioners. Evidently Caesar would protect Cicero if he permitted it.

The tender mercies: It is P. Clodius' intention, when he has achieved plebeian status by adoption and been elected tribune, to prosecute Cicero for having put Roman citizens to death without trial (the Catilinarian conspirators).

Statius: a slave of Quintus, and thought to have too much influence with him. Although Cicero was extremely fond of his brother, at this time propraetor governing the province of Asia, there is no doubt that he found him occasionally unpredictable and irrational.

10 *To Atticus, in N.W. Greece*   *Rome, July, 59 B.C.*

p.44   **The master**: This is more likely to be A. Gabinius (consular candidate for next year, and the giver of the gladiatorial show) or Caesar, rather than Pompey (n. 1). The Latin word is *dominus*.

The Festival of Apollo: an annual festival held at the beginning of July.

The quotations on this page are from an unknown Latin tragedy.

Ye shall rue the very prowess that he showed: This suggests the Romans regretting Pompey's achievements; rather, the address is to the man who had shown the prowess: 'you shall rue . . . that you showed.'

p.45   **Laelius, Furius**: members of the 'Scipionic Circle' (**1, 27**); L. Furius Philus was consul in 136.

Caecilius: Atticus' uncle, and the source of much of his wealth.

Bibulus' edicts: against his colleague Caesar, and no doubt attacking Pompey as well.

11 *To Atticus, at Rome*   *Brindisi, April 29, 58 B.C.*

p.46   **Autronius**: P. Autronius Paetus, elected consul for 65, but convicted of bribery and thus prevented from taking up office. A supporter of Catiline, he was now living in exile in west Greece.

12 *To Terentia, Tullia and young Marcus* *Brindisi, April 29,*
58 B.C.

This is the first of four letters from Cicero to his wife and family from exile. They show him very depressed and pessimistic about the future.

p.47   **Cyzicus**: a town on the Sea of Marmora, the approach to the Black Sea.

Tullia: She was now perhaps twenty-one, recently married to C. Calpurnius Piso Frugi.

Marcus: now about seven years old.

Piso: Tullia's husband. Not to be confused with the consul of this year, L. Calpurnius Piso Caesoninus, whom Cicero viewed as a great enemy.

13 *To Atticus, in N.W. Greece* *Rome, September, 57 B.C.*

p.49   **The Temple of Prosperity near your house**: Atticus' house in Rome was on the Quirinal hill, close to an ancient temple of Prosperity (*Salus*).

The National Assembly: the *comitia centuriata*.

p.50   **My marshal**: i.e. the *nomenclator*, a slave whose task it was to remind his master of the names of those they met.

The Capena Gate: where the Appian Way entered Rome.

Next day I expressed my thanks: This is the extant speech *Post Reditum in Senatu*.

One praetor and two tribunes: The praetor was doubtless Appius Claudius, brother of Cicero's enemy Clodius.

I delivered a speech: perhaps the extant *Post Reditum ad Quirites*.

Messius: C. Messius, tribune of the plebs this year.

Favonius: a republican, supporter of Cato. He was not a consular, so that Cicero is perhaps being ironic in his expression.

For happy though but ill: The line is from Milton, *Paradise Lost* II 224; the similar quotation in Cicero is from an unknown Latin tragedy.

14 *To Atticus, in N.W. Greece*   *Rome, November 23, 57 B.C.*

My porch of Catulus: 'My' is incorrect. The portico, once built by Q. Lutatius Catulus, colleague of C. Marius in the consulship of 102, had been damaged by Clodius when he was destroying Cicero's house adjacent.

The Sacred Way: a street beside the forum at Rome.

Surgery, treatment: Cicero alludes to the suppression of the Catilinarian conspiracy, as often. He no longer wishes to cure the body politic by such traumatic means.

Cermalus hill: part of the Palatine.

Publius Sulla: Like Autronius (**11**), he had been elected to the consulship for 65, but then disqualified for bribery. A prominent but unprincipled man, he was defended by Cicero against a charge of being involved with the Catilinarians, in the speech *Pro Sulla* of 62.

Quintus Flaccus: unknown.

Milo has already taken possession of the election ground: to 'watch the sky' and discern unfavourable omens, in order to stop elections for the curule aedileships for which Clodius was a candidate. Milo was trying to prosecute him for public disorders, and he would be immune from prosecution if he held a magistracy.

Marcellus the candidate: in the same elections. SB thinks this is probably C. Claudius Marcellus, consul of 50.

15 *To Quintus Cicero, in Sardinia Rome, February 15, 56 B.C.*

Quintus is in Sardinia as one of Pompey's legates in the control of corn supplies.

Clodius and Clodia: See p. 38, n. 2.

The constitutionalists: M. Calpurnius Bibulus ('Bibulous' is an unlucky misprint) had been Caesar's frustrated colleague in 59; for Curio, see **9**; for Favonius, **13**; young Servilius is P. Servilius Isauricus, consul in 48.

To enable Pompey to attend: See n. 2. More probably, however, the reason was that Pompey could not properly enter the city while he held *imperium* (to deal with the corn crisis).

Cato: This is not the famous M. Porcius Cato, but a relative, C. Porcius Cato, a troublesome tribune of this year.

p.54   **Reproaching Pompey for his treachery**: in allowing Cicero to be hounded into exile in 58.

Scipio Africanus, Gaius Carbo: The great Scipio Aemilianus (**1**) was found dead in bed one morning in 129, when he was due to address the Senate that day on the rights of the Italian allies; responsibility was never proved, but some ascribed the deed to C. Papirius Carbo, a leading politician of the time. Pompey claims to take that view.

Has sent for men from the country districts: Pompey had strong family influence in Picenum, north east Italy; there could also be his veteran soldiers, now settled on the land.

Cato's proposal: C. Cato (see above) supported Clodius. He had promulgated a bill against Milo, the contents of which are not known, and proposed the recall of P. Lentulus Spinther (see **20**) from his province; it is not known on what grounds.

16 *To Atticus, on his way to Rome*   *Anzio, April, 56 B.C.*

Those two shows you gave: Atticus would not himself give gladiatorial shows; he would hire the troop out. Cicero's language suggests that there is a joke of some kind here.

17 *To Atticus, at Rome*   *Anzio, May, 56 B.C.*

p.55   **The man I sent them to**: presumably Pompey. Great pressure was put on Cicero after the triumvirs had patched up their differences at Luca; on this one should see the letter to Lentulus Spinther in December 54, *Ad Fam.* I 9.9.

It appears that Cicero's brother Quintus had made certain undertakings to Pompey to persuade him to facilitate Cicero's return from exile in 57, and Pompey now demanded their fulfilment.

My 'palinode': i.e. recantation (the term comes from a story about the Greek lyric poet Stesichorus, who wrote a poem criticising Helen and went blind; he then wrote a second poem, recanting, and recovered his sight). Cicero's palinode was probably his speech *De Provinciis Consularibus*, on the provinces to be allotted to the consuls of 55 (now to be Pompey and Crassus); in it he praises Caesar enthusiastically.

Those 'leaders': not the triumvirs, but the leaders of the senate, the optimates, who Cicero believed (no doubt correctly) had always let him down.

p.56 **apotheosis**: 'deification', i.e. exaggerated praise of Caesar.

A house that once belonged to Catulus: This was Cicero's villa at Tusculum, not his town house, which is referred to later in this sentence. For Catulus, see **14**.

Vettius: the notorious informer about an alleged plot to kill Pompey in 59 (*Ad Att*. II 24.2).

18 *To Lucius Lucceius*   *Anzio, May, 56 B.C.*

Lucius Lucceius was a friend of Cicero who had been praetor in 67 and an unsuccessful candidate for the consulship in 59. He had turned to the writing of history. This letter, asking Lucceius to compose a history of Cicero's consulship, exile and return (i.e. from before 63 to 57) angled to present the protagonist in the best possible light, has been seen in the past as discreditable to Cicero, and perhaps to our minds it is. We should however realise that the writing of history in the Roman world was more of an art than a science, and a rhetorical flavour was not at all inappropriate (cf. Livy, Tacitus). Cicero himself thought this an exceedingly well written letter (p. 59); he would not have expected the modern objections.

p.57 **The Italian and Civil Wars**: The Italian would be what we

20

call the Social War (91–88), the Civil that between Sulla and Marius (and Cinna; 88–82).

Many Greeks have done: Callisthenes was a historian of Alexander the Great; the Phocian War is more commonly called the Sacred War (356–346). Timaeus was famous for a history of Sicily; the War of Pyrrhus would deal with his invasion of Italy in 281–275. Polybius, the great Hellenistic historian, a friend of Scipio Aemilianus at Rome, composed a history from 264 to 146, of which large parts are extant. Nothing apart from this reference is known of a monograph by him on Scipio's siege of Numantia (133) which brought to an end a long period of war in Spain. For historians concentrating on a single narrow subject, we may compare Sallust's *Jugurtha* and *Catiline*, and Tacitus' *Agricola*.

Xenophon's Hercules: This refers to the famous allegorical story of the choice of Hercules between two beautiful women representing Pleasure and Virtue (Xenophon, *Memorabilia* II 1.21–33).

p.58   **Epaminondas**: See n. 1 below.

The exile and return of Themistocles: Themistocles did not return alive. He was the architect of the Athenian victory at Salamis in 480, but got into trouble with the democracy after the war, and went into exile in Persia itself. After his death his body was secretly brought back to Athens (Thucydides I 138.6); so in fact he did return.

19 *To Atticus, at Rome*   *In the country, May, 56 B.C.*

Lentulus Niger: a distinguished member of an important family; priest of Mars, he had stood unsuccessfully for the consulship of 58.

Saufeius: a wealthy friend of Atticus, who had written on the Epicurean philosophy.

p.59   **To arms and fight**: It is clear from this and other hints that there was considerable if muted opposition to the triumvirs in the senate during this year, even after the re-establishment of their domination at Luca.

Philoxenus: The story is that Dionysius I, tyrant of Syracuse, had written tragedies, which he showed to a poet called Philoxenus, who did not find it possible to praise them and was sent to the stone mines. Later he was released and brought back to court, and asked for his opinion of the tyrant's compositions: 'Take me back to the mines', he said.

20 *To Lentulus Spinther,*
  Governor of Cilicia   *Rome, late August, 56 B.C.*

P. Cornelius Lentulus Spinther, consul of 57, had played a large part in Cicero's recall from exile, for which Cicero felt a deep debt of gratitude. *Ad Fam.* I 1–9 is a sequence of letters written to him in his proconsular province, in the years 56 to 54. The biggest single question discussed in them is that of the restoration of Ptolemy Auletes to the throne of Egypt (p. 53, n. 1). Lentulus, being on the spot, as governor of Cilicia, hoped and expected to be given the commission to do this; but there was great competition, including the suggestion that Pompey himself coveted it (**15**). Eventually A. Gabinius, governor of Syria, took the matter into his own hands, and restored the king in 55 (**22**).

21 *To Lentulus Spinther,*
  Governor of Cilicia   *Rome, January, 55 B.C.*

p.60   **M. Plaetorius**: not known.

22 *To Atticus, at Rome*   *Cuma, near Naples, April 22, 55 B.C.*

p.61   **Ptolemy has been restored**: See note on **20**.
  Faustus: a son of the dictator Sulla. It is presumed that Faustus had sold his library to Cicero, and that it contained books brought back by his father from Greece and Asia.
  The presidential chair: i.e. the *sella curulis*, the seat of the high magistrates at Rome.

22

23 *To Marcus Marius, near Naples   Rome, September, 55 B.C.*

This famous letter describes the lavish public games given by Pompey as consul at the dedication of his new theatre. Marius was a friend of Cicero, of less than robust health, who lived near Naples.

p.62   **Spurius Maecius** (Tarpa): He had some special position in connection with the choice of plays for public performances; and is referred to twice by Horace in the same context (*Sat.* I 10.38, *Ars Poetica* 387).

Aesopus: the most famous tragic actor of the time.

Protogenes: evidently an *anagnostes* (a slave with the task of reading aloud) belonging to Marius.

Oscan farces: We call them Atellan farce, a form of native Italian comedy which probably influenced Plautus.

Greek Street: an evident joke. We know nothing about where it was.

You who scorned the gladiators: Perhaps as T/P think, Marius had helped Cicero in the past, during his troubles with Clodius and his gang.

p.63   **Caninius Gallus**: He had been tribune in 56, a supporter of Pompey.

24 *To Julius Caesar, in Gaul   Rome, Spring, 54 B.C.*

A letter from Cicero to Caesar, recommending his close friend C. Trebatius Testa, a famous jurist, for a position on Caesar's staff in Gaul.

p.64   **Now that Pompey has delayed**: Pompey is now pro-consular governor of Spain for five years. He is however staying in Italy. Cicero expected to be appointed a legate on Pompey's staff, as he had been in the corn supply crisis of 57.

For reasons not unknown to you: It is supposed that Cicero refers to some threat from Clodius. Alternatively, he may simply mean that Caesar is aware of a certain indecisiveness in his character.

Marcus (?) Orfius: SB convincingly argues that the man in question, whose name is corruptly given in the manuscripts, must be M. Curtius (see bottom of p. 65). Cicero had asked Caesar to appoint him military tribune.

Lepta: later with Cicero in Cilicia (*Ad Fam.* III 7.4).

My letter concerning Milo: It is difficult to imagine why Cicero should have written to Caesar about Milo, who had violently opposed the triumvirs and their supporters; nor of course do we know the 'cliché' he had used.

The rank of colonel: The Latin word is *tribunatum*, 'the position of military tribune', an army officer of middle rank, between the prefect in command of a legion and the centurions.

25 *To Quintus Cicero, in Gaul*   *Rome, June 3, 54 B.C.*

Quintus, by agreement between his brother and himself, had gone to join Caesar's staff in Gaul.

p.65   **The rank of Colonel for Marcus Curtius**: See on **24**.

p.66   **Some hope of elections**: The letters of this and the following months are full of the scandals of the coming consular elections, in which all four candidates were being accused of bribery.

Some idea of a dictatorship: This would be Pompey. The dictatorship was a traditional office, a temporary appointment in a crisis, involving the suspension of the normal consular government.

These are the fruits: Euripides, *Suppliants* 119.

26 *To Quintus Cicero, in Britain*   *Arpino, September 28,*
54 B.C.

p.67   **Laterium**: a village near Arpino, where Quintus had an estate.

The temple of Furina: an ancient goddess, with a temple also in Rome.

Varro: This may well be the scholar M. Terentius Varro **(87, 109)**.

p.68   **Scipio Africanus**: See **1**. These members of the 'Scipionic circle' are indeed the interlocutors in the *Republic* as it has reached us, not by the normal process of manuscripts copied down through the Middle Ages (apart from the famous *Dream of Scipio* which formed the finale), but by its discovery on a palimpsest in the early nineteenth century; about a third is now extant. So Cicero's plan for a change of speakers put forward in this letter was not put into effect.

Nine books: Change was made in this respect, for the work was in fact published in six books (**47**).

Sallust: Cicero's friend Cn. Sallustius, not the historian C. Sallustius Crispus. This is probably the same man whose loyalty is praised in **12**.

Heraclides Ponticus: a philosopher, pupil of Plato. He wrote dialogues, choosing interlocutors who were long dead.

My work on the principles of rhetoric: The *De Oratore* (*On the Orator*), Cicero's longest and most important rhetorical treatise, published in 55.

On the Republic* and *On Individual Eminence: Aristotle wrote dialogues which have not survived. This *On the Republic* is not the extant *Politics*, which is not a dialogue, but a lost work called *Politicus*. *On Individual Eminence* may be an alternative description of the same work (in which case the translation is at fault), or else another lost dialogue.

Four tragedies in sixteen days: Quintus, like his brother, had strong literary interests. *Electra* and *Trojan Women* are familiar to us as subjects for tragedy; *Erigone* involves an obscure Attic myth.

28 *To Trebatius Testa, in Gaul   Rome, December, 54 B.C.*

For Trebatius, see **24**.

p.69   **Mucius and Manilius**: These were the names of famous legal authorities. But, as SB says, Cicero must also be referring to common friends of Trebatius and himself. A Manilius is mentioned in another letter to Trebatius

(*Ad Fam.* VII 8.2), and there was a Mucius Scaevola who was tribune of the plebs in this year (*Ad Att.* IV 17.4).
Comfort or counsel: Terence, *The Self-Tormentor* 86.

29 *To Atticus, at Rome*   *?Minturnae, May, 51 B.C.*

p.71   **I'll look after the boys**: i.e. the male slaves on the farm; but commentators have found it difficult to imagine the situation and why Pomponia found Quintus' remark offensive.
Statius: Quintus' freedman.

p.72   **Aulus** (Manlius) **Torquatus**: a distinguished Roman, praetor in 70, and a close friend of Cicero (*Ad Fam.* VI 1–4).

30 *To Cicero, from Marcus Caelius*   *Rome, late in May, 51 B.C.*

Cicero's governorship of Cilicia in 51 and 50 was enlivened by his correspondence with M. Caelius Rufus, a brilliant and amiable young man defended by Cicero in the speech *Pro Caelio* of 56, and an incisive political commentator. Caelius' letters, seventeen in number, fill *Ad Fam.* VIII; Cicero's replies are in *Ad Fam.* II 8–16.
Rumours about elections north of the Po: This refers to Caesar's long held plan to extend Roman citizenship to Cisalpine Gaul. For the time being it is only a rumour.
Marcellus: the consul, M. Claudius Marcellus.
Proposal about the succession to the governorship of Gaul: See *Introduction*, pp. 4–6.

p.73   **The same opinion**: no doubt that he was ineffective.
Domitius: consul 54, a vehement anti-Caesarian.
Quintus Pompeius: Q. Pompeius Rufus was tribune in 52, a supporter of Clodius against Milo. He was condemned to exile for the riots which followed Clodius' death.
Your friend Plancus: T. Munatius Plancus Bursa, also

tribune in 52, and prosecuted by Cicero himself for his part in the rioting after Clodius' death. 'Your friend' is sarcastic.

31 *To Atticus* *Athens, June 29, 51 B.C.*

Pomptinus: C. Pomptinus, praetor 63. Cicero's chief of staff in Cilicia.

p.74 **Caesar's Law**: Passed during Caesar's consulship, it limited the requisitions a governor could make when travelling officially.

A chacun son métier: The Greek proverb, quoted by Aristophanes at *Wasps* 1431, means 'let each man stick to the job he understands'.

Aristus: currently head of the New Academy (successor to the school of philosophy founded by Plato) in Athens. He succeeded his brother Antiochus of Ascalon (**109, 111**) in this position.

I haven't let Quintus: rather, 'I have left Xeno to Quintus'. Xeno was a close friend of Atticus in Athens, perhaps therefore an Epicurean.

32 *To Gaius Memmius, at Mitylene* *Athens, end of June, 51 B.C.*

p.75 **The injustice you suffered**: C. Memmius had been one of the four candidates for the consulship of 53, all of whom had been accused of bribery (**25**). He was now living in exile in Athens.

Patro: the current head of the Epicurean school; his predecessor was Phaedrus (below).

I differ from him violently: Cicero is always scornful of Epicureanism, both because he considers hedonism un-Roman and because he thinks the Epicureans unintellectual.

Privileges and remunerations: Most probably T/P interpret this rightly, that there were some *honoraria* due to Patro for his teaching at Rome, which Cicero aided him in recovering.

Phaedrus: See above.

Philo: head of the New Academy before Antiochus (**31**). Cicero had known him well in Rome in the early 80's.

27

I know the race: i.e. The Greeks, whom as individuals the Romans despised.

You had abandoned that particular building project: Evidently Memmius owned the site of Epicurus' house, and had been intending to build there himself.

p.76 **Or the Areopagus**: This is a misprint for 'of'. The Areopagus was the ancient court of Athens. It appears that Memmius has received building permission from the Areopagus, overruling the terms of Epicurus' will (cf. 'the rights of testators' above). The Epicurean authorities request his permission to get that decision revoked.

33 *To Caelius, at Rome*   *Athens, July 6, 51 B.C.*

This is Cicero's reply to Caelius' letter (**30**).

p.77 **Give him thyself**: The Latin words form a rough hexameter, and so are thought by some to be a quotation, and if so probably from the satirist Lucilius; but they may not be a quotation at all.

34 *To Atticus, at Rome*   *Isle of Delos, July 12, 51 B.C.*

Delos: an important market at this time, and a natural stopping-place for Roman travellers to Asia.

Cape Lombarda: anciently Zoster, a promontory not far along the coast from the Piraeus.

'The promontories of Gyrae': The phrase comes from the early lyric poet Archilochus (fr. 105 West).

35 *To Atticus, at Rome*   *Ephesus, late in July, 51 B.C.*

Cicero has now reached Ephesus on the coast of Asia Minor, on his way to his province of Cilicia far to the south-east. (See map on p. 158.) Delegations from the province are already there to meet him.

p.78 **Appius**: Appius Claudius Pulcher, consul 54, was Cicero's predecessor in Cilicia. He was brother of Cicero's enemy Clodius.

37 *To Cicero, from Caelius* *Rome, August 1, 51 B.C.*

p.79 **The temple of Apollo**: outside the city boundary; cf. **15**.

Pay for Pompey's troops: in Spain or about to go. Some had presumably been enrolled in the north-east, and were now at Rimini (Ariminum); see below.

That legion: raised by Pompey in Cisalpine Gaul and lent to Caesar in 52. (For the later history, see **67**.)

The appointment of Caesar's successor: See *Introduction*, pp. 4−6.

Paullus: L. Aemilius Paullus, consul elect, brother of M. Lepidus the triumvir of 43. The consul elect spoke first in debates in the Senate.

Sittius' bond: Presumably this was a debt owned to Sittius in Cilicia, in which Caelius had an interest. He expects Cicero to enforce payment.

The panthers: Caelius wanted Cicero to get some panthers for him, for public games he expected to give as aedile the following year.

The King of Alexandria: The same Ptolemy whom Gabinius restored in 55 (**22**).

38 *To Atticus* *Laodicea, August 3, 51 B.C.*

Laodicea, though not in Cilicia proper, was included in the Roman province; as also was the island of Cyprus (**46**, **47**).

Aulus Plotius: praetor at Rome this year.

Our friend Caesar: The Latin merely says 'our friend'. SB thinks it is more likely to be Pompey.

p.80 **Your runaway slave**: Presumably a slave of Atticus had absconded and joined this brigand.

Talk about an ox with panniers: proverbial for somebody

trying to do a job for which he is not fitted. The line comes from an unknown Latin comedy.

39 *To Atticus, at Rome*   *In camp, Synnas, August, 51 B.C.*

Devastated: by the misgovernment and peculation of previous governors, especially Appius.

p.81   **Not a man but some wild beast**: Appius.
Caesar's Law: See **31**.
He's holding assizes: This is improper behaviour with his successor already in the province.
Bibulus: He also (consul 59) had been caught by the new provisions (p. 70), and sent as governor to Syria.

40 *To Appius, at Tarsus*   *Iconium, August 29, 51 B.C.*

Book III of *Ad Fam.* consists of thirteen letters from Cicero to Appius Claudius. The present one remonstrates with him for his extremely rude behaviour to his successor as governor. No doubt Appius, being of ancient patrician family, did not care what Cicero thought of him.
When I compare: The translation of this sentence is more unfriendly than Cicero's Latin, but no doubt this is what he meant.
Phania: a freedman of Appius.

p.82   **Sulla's Law**: on the arrangements for the governing of the provinces.

p.83   **To Cilicia**: i.e. Cilicia proper; the province included other districts.

41 *To Cicero, from Caelius*   *Rome, September 2, 51 B.C.*

Patiscus: a businessman in Cilicia.

He only gives away country houses: We do not know what Caelius is referring to; but Curio was an extravagant man.

42 *To Cicero, from Caelius*   *Rome, October, 51 B.C.*

p.84   **Before March 1**: See *Introduction*, pp. 4−6.

43 *To Caelius, at Rome*   *Before Pindenissus, November 14,*
51 B.C.

p.85   **Hillus**: C. Lucilius Hirrus, tribune in 53, had failed at the elections where Caelius succeeded.

Our Cassius: C. Cassius Longinus, the tyrannicide. Cicero knew him well. He was in Syria with the remains of Crassus' army (defeated at Carrhae in 53). He successfully repelled Parthian invasions of Syria in 52 and 51.

Issus: the site of Alexander the Great's victory in 333 B.C. Clitarchus was Alexander's historian.

44 *To Cicero, from Caelius*   *Rome, February, 50 B.C.*

p.86   **Appius has been impeached by Dolabella**: The charge is unknown, but evidently involved illegality in connection with his province. P. Cornelius Dolabella appears for the first time. He was a very young man, born in 69 according to Appian (*Bell. Civ.* II 129), and, if so, only nineteen years old at this time. (SB however argues that he was older than this, perhaps twenty-five; see **54**.) Dolabella plays a major rôle from now on, both in the politics of Rome and as Cicero's son-in-law, third husband of Tullia.

p.87   **One or other of his sons**: Gnaeus and Sextus.

If I wasn't having a fight: as aedile, responsible for the civic administration at Rome.

31

P.S. – I said that Curio: This is evidently the moment of Curio's notorious switch to Caesar, against whom he had been most active before.

He failed in the matter of the leap-month: The Roman calendar, before Caesar's reform, only allowed for 355 days in the year. Consequently it was necessary to insert an 'intercalary month' of some twenty days every second year. But the decision had to be taken each time, by the College of Priests. There should have been an intercalary month after 23rd February in 50, and apparently Curio was pressing for it. The question had political significance, because an intercalary month would have delayed the important discussion of the consular provinces on March 1st.

Rullus' Land Bill: blocked by Cicero when consul in 63. The comparison probably lies in the wide powers conferred on the commission to be set up to implement the bill.

45 *To Appius*   *Laodicea, February, 50 B.C.*

Appius Claudius has now got back to Rome.

p.88   **The matter of my distinction**: i.e. Cicero's hope of a triumph for his military successes in Cilicia.

Your triumph: As we have already learned from Caelius (**44**), Appius had shrewdly decided to discard this ambition.

46 *To Atticus, in N.W. Greece   Laodicea, February 13, 50 B.C.*

p.90   **If follows that this bond was now on exactly the same footing as any other**: This was Cicero's legal ruling, that the senatorial decree and the later rider exempted the present transaction from the terms of the Gabinian Law, but did not overrule other legal provisions. Thus Cicero protected the Salaminians from 48% interest.

p.91   **His uncle Cato**: Cato was half-brother of Brutus' mother Servilia.

47 *To Atticus*   *Laodicea, February 24, 50 B.C.*

For two years: This must be from the latest renewal of the loan. The original loan was made in 56 B.C. (p. 90).

Its patron Cato and Brutus himself: Cato was sent to Cyprus in 58 to take over the island. He stayed until 56, as did Brutus who accompanied him. No doubt this was the origin of the loan.

p.92   **Paullus**: the consul of this year.

Scaptius had been duly and lawfully paid: i.e. so far as Cicero's legal ruling went; Scaptius' refusal to take the money was a gamble on the future.

Communities' contributions: Provincial communities had in the past contributed to the cost of games at Rome.

48 *To Caelius, at Rome*   *Laodicea, April 4, 50 B.C.*

p.93   **The festival of the Great Mother**: the *ludi Megalenses*, in honour of Cybele, held April 4–10.

49 *To Atticus*   *Laodicea, early May, 50 B.C.*

p.94   **Those old battles of mine**: i.e. when, as a candidate for elected office in Rome, he made himself available to all citizens from the earliest morning.

50 *To Cicero, from Cato*   *Rome, May, 50 B.C.*

This is the only letter in the collection to Cicero from the austere Marcus Porcius Cato.

p.95   **King Ariobarzanes**: King of Cappadocia, neighbour to Cilicia.

51 *To Caelius, at Rome*   *In Cilicia, June, 50 B.C.*

Rowdy elections: rather, 'rowdy public meetings'.
Spring Vacation: the Quinquatrus, a festival of Minerva held from March 19 to 23. Curio as tribune was vetoing the discussion of the consular provinces (in the interests of Caesar), and this had led to public disturbances.
There *were* **many things**: rather, 'there are'.

p.96   **Pessinus**: in central Asia Minor (see map, p. 158).
Philo: A freedman of Caelius.

52 *To Atticus, in N.W. Greece*   *In Cilicia, June, 50 B.C.*

Wide seas betwixt us lie: from an unknown Greek poet.
My quaestor: one L. Mescinius Rufus. Quaestors were in charge of financial affairs in a province.

p.97   **Thesprotia and Chaonia**: districts of North West Greece, where Atticus chose to live.

53 *To Cicero, from Caelius*   *Rome, June, 50 B.C.*

Caesar should retire on November 13: See *Introduction*, pp. 4–6. This is a particular day, the Ides of November.
Our friends: the optimates.
His second consulship: in 55.
Caesar will come to the help of his vetoing tribune: as indeed he did at the beginning of 49.

54 *To Cicero, from Caelius*   *Rome, June, 50 B.C.*

p.98   **With maturity**: This phrase is SB's strongest argument for questioning Appian's date of 69 for the birth of Dolabella (**44**). He suggests rather that he was now about twenty-five years old.

Curio's veto regarding the provinces: This was foreseen; see **42**.

The question of the veto was discussed: The senate had decided in advance (as in some other cases) that if a tribune used his veto on this matter, that action itself should immediately be discussed.

Marcellus spoke first: This was M. Marcellus, consul of the previous year.

In exactly the opposite sense: i.e. they wanted to compromise with Caesar.

Pompey the 'Great': Pompey was seriously ill during this year.

---

55 *To Caelius, at Rome*   *Side, early August, 50 B.C.*

A good friend: i.e. to Curio.

Your namesake Caelius: in fact this was one C. Coelius Caldus, who came out to Cilicia as replacement for Mescinius Rufus (**52**).

p.99 **Governor of West Asia Minor**: Quintus held this office from 61 to 58, after his praetorship in 62.

In a constant state of uneasiness: The reference for the information in n. 1 below is *Ad Att.* VI 6.4.

The two most powerful people: Pompey and Caesar.

Cassius or Antonius: Quaestors were normally allocated to provincial governors by lot. But Pompey had chosen Q. Cassius Longinus (brother or cousin of the tyrannicide C. Cassius) as his quaestor in Spain in about 52 B.C., and Caesar chose M. Antonius (Mark Antony) as his quaestor in Gaul.

---

56 *To Atticus*   *Rhodes, about August 10, 50 B.C.*

Tiberius Nero: Tiberius Claudius Nero, a young patrician, later husband of Livia and father of the emperor Tiberius.

Any any rate: Read, 'at any rate'.

This letter answers Cato's (**50**).

Glad I am: Hector to his father Priam in a tragedy by Naevius, the powerful Latin writer of the end of the third century (earlier than Plautus), who composed comedy, tragedy and epic. Cicero is very fond of this quotation, 'I think' being merely to avoid an appearance of pedantry.

That you willingly conceded: When one works it out, one sees that this is not a particularly grateful remark.

58 *To Cicero, from Caelius* *Rome, early August, 50 B.C.*

This letter is an invaluable contemporary assessment of the political situation by a quick and perceptive (and unprincipled) man.

p.100 **That both should give up their armies**: This proposal was put forward by Curio and carried by the Senate, but Pompey refused to accept it (see p. 105).

p.101 **The judiciary**: i.e. those who sit on juries, the wealthier classes in the state (senate, knights and tribunes of the treasury; see **4**).

I only hope we have time enough: rather, 'to be sure, there is time enough'.

Appius as censor: Two censors were elected every five years, normally from among the ex-consuls, to review the citizen body, enquire into behaviour in public life, and take appropriate action. Appius Claudius' colleague was L. Calpurnius Piso, consul in 58.

Drusus: M. Livius Drusus Claudianus, father of Livia, the future wife of Augustus. A *Lex Scantinia* penalised acts of homosexuality between free men; Caelius suggests that Drusus, praetor this year, is a grotesque choice for somebody to preside over a trial under that law; but Caelius may have had private reasons for dissatisfaction on this, as it is he himself who has recently been accused under the *Lex Scantinia* (*Ad Fam.* VIII 12.3).

Appius: who had plundered the province from which he had just returned.

p.102   **From the outset**: These are the key words. If Cicero had listened to Atticus earlier, he would have been saved personal anguish (exile). He only came round to the triumvirs in 56.

But never didst thou: *Odyssey* 9.33, modified.

p.103   **'Think of the vows'**: apparently a quotation, meaning 'what is to come of all my pledges and promises (if I oppose Caesar now on this question)?'

When he asked me: This explains the 'vows'. Although he never says so elsewhere, it appears that Cicero had visited Caesar at Ravenna (the nearest point of his province) probably in the winter of 53/52, and agreed to persuade Caelius (tribune in 52) to support the proposal that Caesar should be allowed to stand for the consulship in absence. If so, he was successful, because a bill was passed in 52, called the Law of the Ten Tribunes, giving Caesar exactly this exemption from the normal rules.

That wonderful third consulship: This must be sarcastic.

I fear reproach: This is another favourite quotation of Cicero, taken from the words of Hector in his soliloquy at *Iliad* 22.105 and 100. (Hector fears public loss of honour if he takes refuge in the city; Polydamas advised a safe return in Book XVIII and Hector, by refusing and keeping the army out on the plain, has lost many Trojan lives. So it seems best to him to stay where he is and fight Achilles.)

To let a fool: apparently the same proverb as our 'fools rush in where angels fear to tread'.

My Triumph: The magistrate who was waiting for a triumph was not allowed to enter Rome, because he still held his imperium, and was accompanied by his lictors. Cicero thinks of using this to avoid attending senate meetings; and indeed he kept those lictors with him for another couple of years, still hoping for a triumph (**81**).

That show of virtue: He means that his staff in Cilicia had been pretending to agree with his high principles, but had failed to keep it up.

My quaestor: Coelius (**55**).

Thucydides: Book I 97, referring to his famous digression on the *Pentekontaetia*.

Was ready to vote for more: See his letter (**50**).
Favonius: **13**.
Hirrus: **43**.
n. 1: The reference for the information given here is *Ad Att.* VII 2.7.

61 *To Tiro, at Patras*   *Leucas, November 7, 50 B.C.*

Tiro, Cicero's secretary, seems to have enjoyed poor health. Cicero and his brother Quintus always write to him in most friendly terms, and with sympathetic concern. He outlived Cicero and his brother by nearly forty years (p. 76).

62 *To Atticus*   *Pompeii, December 10, 50 B.C.*

Hirtius: A. Hirtius, Caesarian, will be mentioned frequently from now on.
Scipio: the consul of 52. Pompey married his daughter after the death of Julia in 54 B.C.

63 *To Atticus, at Rome*   *Formia, December 18, 50 B.C.*

If negotiations had been begun with him: The senate could have formally requested that the consuls take the matter up with the vetoing tribune, and this would have put heavy pressure on Curio, but the senate voted against doing so (**54**).
The squandering of the Campanian allotments: The *ager Campanus* was the central issue in the dispute between the triumvirs and their opponents. It had been allocated to Pompey's veterans by Caesar in his consulship, by the Land Bill (**9**) forced through the popular assembly as the senate would not approve it. The opposition argued that it was using up the only free public land in Italy, and so depriving the state of rents. When attempts were made in later years to stand up against the triumvirs, reconsideration of the *ager Campanus* was the rallying cry (*Ad Fam.* I 9.8).

p.107 **The adoption of a patrician by a plebeian**: Clodius, adopted by P. Fonteius, a plebeian, so that he should be eligible to become tribune of the plebs; this happened in 59, sanctioned by Caesar as *Pontifex Maximus*, with the concurrence of Pompey as augur.

A citizen of Cadiz: Balbus was adopted by Pompey's friend Theophanes of Mytilene.

Labienus: chief lieutenant of Caesar in Gaul; see **65**.

Mamurra: Caesar's chief of engineers in Gaul, attacked by Catullus (Poems 29, 57).

Let him stand in accordance with the law: This would be the Law of the Ten Tribunes (**60**).

Outlawed: He means proscribed, put to death without trial.

You'll still be slaves: because the alternative to domination by Caesar will be domination by Pompey.

Cinna: who, with Marius, massacred the optimates in 86.

Sulla: who instituted the first proscription in 81.

Alexis: a Greek slave of Atticus.

64 *To Tiro, at Patras*   *Near Rome, January 12, 49 B.C.*

p.108 **Mark Antony and Quintus Cassius**: now tribunes.

With Curio: also Caelius, though Cicero for some reason does not mention him.

p.109 **Capua**: Cicero is in charge of the defence of the coast of Campania, an important responsibility.

65 *To Tiro, at Patras   Capua, near Naples, January 27, 49 B.C.*

p.110 **Rimini, Pesaro, Ancona and Arezzo**: See map on p. 29. Arezzo is in the centre of Italy, on the way to Rome; the other three cities are strung out down the Adriatic coast. Caesar has moved fast after crossing the Rubicon.

The following terms: These seem to give as much as the senate could ask. But he can hardly have expected them to be accepted; and when the senate tried to lay down conditions in return, it was easy enough to drag the matter out, and in the meantime consolidate his position.

Pompey to go to Spain: to his province, which he has been irregularly governing through legates, Afranius (consul in 60) and Petreius named later in this letter. There were reliable legions there, but they were not at hand to help in Italy.

Further Gaul to Domitius: L. Domitius Ahenobarbus (consul 54) had been given the province of Transalpine Gaul by the senate, M. Considius (who had been praetor) that of Cisalpine Gaul.

Titus Labienus: See **63**. He refused to be a party to the invasion of his homeland, and left Caesar when he crossed the Rubicon. He fought to the end against him.

Dolabella: husband of Tullia. His presence in Caesar's army was an embarrassment to Cicero, who might be accused by the Pompeians of keeping his options open.

66 *To Atticus, at Rome*   *Formia, February 2, 49 B.C.*

p.111 **In case none of us should be there**: i.e. none of the ex-consuls.

Had raised no forces: Cicero does not think it advisable to mention his official responsibilities around Capua.

67 *To Atticus, at Rome*   *Capua, near Naples, February 5, 49 B.C.*

Nothing matters less to these consuls: rather, 'nothing is more worthless than these consuls'.

I came to Capua as instructed: He had been asked by the consuls to be at Capua on February 5th for a meeting.

Lucera: This was Pompey's base, chosen (as Cicero later notes, **69**) to facilitate a withdrawal to Brindisi and across to Greece if that became advisable.

Units of Appius' not very reliable legions were approaching: rather, 'he was visiting the units . . .'. 'Appius' legions' were the only two legions in Italy at Pompey's disposal. He had lent one legion to Caesar three years ago, for a crisis in

Gaul (**37**). In 50 the senate required each of the commanders to return one legion to Italy for use against the Parthians (Cicero has mentioned the threat of an invasion of the eastern provinces); Pompey offered the one he had lent to Caesar, and Caesar had acquiesced, sending therefore two. The Parthian threat had evaporated, and the legions had not gone to the east. However, their loyalty was uncertain; Pompey did not feel that he could trust them to fight against their old commander, at least until a period of time had elapsed and they had been retrained. It is supposed that they are called Appius' legions because an Appius Claudius, probably nephew of Cicero's predecessor in Cilicia, had brought them to Italy from Gaul.

'To every man upon this earth (death cometh soon or late)': The quotation is taken by Wilkinson from Macaulay's *How Horatius kept the Bridge*. Cicero uses the first couple of words of a Greek quotation, indicating that he would be willing to die in defence of Italy.

My bodyguard: These are the lictors whom Cicero still kept by him, in the hope of being awarded a triumph (**60**).

p.112   **A Phalaris or a Pisistratus**: Phalaris was the cruel tyrant of Acragas in Sicily, notorious for roasting his enemies in a bronze bull; Pisistratus the tyrant of Athens who made it a cultural centre. Both lived in the sixth century.

At Formia: i.e. at his villa there.

68 *To Pompey, at Lucera*   *Formia, February 16, 49 B.C.*

This letter from Cicero to Pompey is preserved among the letters to Atticus, not those *Ad Familiares*. The reason is that Cicero sent Atticus a copy. Various important official and semi-official communications about this time are preserved in this way, including also letters from Pompey to Cicero, and from Pompey to the consuls and to Domitius, the commander in the north. *Ad Att.* VIII 11 has four such enclosures, and so does VIII 12.

Vibullius: He seems to have been the one senatorial commander who acted with resolution and some success against Caesar's troops. He commanded a number of cohorts which had been raised in Picenum, in Pompeian territory.

Lucius Torquatus: L. Manlius Torquatus, son of the consul of 65.

69 *To Atticus, at Rome*   *Formia, February 16, 49 B.C.*

p.113   **Domitius' levy**: L. Domitius Ahenobarbus, inveterate enemy of Caesar, had as proconsul overall command of the senatorial forces in the north, facing Caesar. He is remote from Pompey's control, and soon after this gets himself cut off in the town of Corfinium (Popoli on the map, p. 29), and is forced to surrender, thus losing both his own cohorts and those of Vibullius, who had joined him, the only really reliable troops available to Pompey.

Such glowing colours as Philotimus: *Ad Att.* VII 23, written on February 10, quotes a letter from Philotimus (a freedman of Terentia's) with inaccurately optimistic news from the north.

The man who abandoned the head itself: i.e. Rome.

I replied at once: in Letter **68**. It is interesting to see how Cicero modifies what he said in reporting it to Atticus.

To endure with reputed loyalists: What Cicero means is that he must join the loyalists (the *boni*) for the sake of his public image, even though he considers that they are not really loyal at that. Many of them are now making their way backs to Rome.

Lepidus, Volcacius, Sulpicius: all ex-consuls.

70 *To Atticus, at Rome*   *Calvi, February 18, 49 B.C.*

p.114   **I took steps long ago**: by his support since 56, and by sending his brother Quintus to serve on Caesar's staff.

Will moreover be in danger: Cicero does not wholly trust Pompey either; the fear of a Sullan proscription if Pompey returned victorious from the east was in people's minds.

p.115   The first half of this page has a most useful summary of the unconstitutional and illegal acts of the past decade, including some for which this is prime historical evidence.

Passing laws by force when the omens were unfavourable: in Caesar's consulship in 59, when he rudely disregarded the attempts by his colleague Bibulus to use the established religious safeguards of the constitution.

In his third consulship: in 52. Here we have the mention of the Law of the Ten Tribunes, and of a bill passed by Pompey himself, confirming Caesar's exemption from the requirement to stand in person for the consulship.

Opposed the consul Marcus Marcellus when he was for fixing March 1 as the closing date for Caesar's governship: See *Introduction*, pp. 4—6, and cf. **30**. Extraordinarily, it remains uncertain whether this refers to March 50 or March 49.

71 *To Atticus, at Rome*   *Formia, February 25, 49 B.C.*

The reference for this letter should be *Ad Att.* VIII 9.4; Letter **76** is VIII 9.1—3.

p.116   **Reign of Terror**: probably an allusion to the terror under Cinna after the departure of Sulla (cf. **63**).

p.117   **This instrument of wrath**: Caesar.

72 *To Atticus, at Rome*   *Formia, March 1, 49 B.C.*

The Straits: i.e. the Adriatic. From Brindisi is the shortest crossing to Greece.

73 *To Atticus, at Rome*   *Formia, March 11, 49 B.C.*

The six battalions (i.e. cohorts, of which there were ten to a legion) **which were at Alba**: These were senatorial troops which now changed sides, and joined Caesar's cavalry commander Vibius Curius (Caesar, *Civil War* I 24).

p.118   **Lucius Metellus the tribune**: son of the consul of 68. Metellus returned to Rome soon after this and annoyed Caesar by attempting to use his tribunician veto (**78**).

His mother-in-law Clodia: one of the three sisters of Appius Claudius.

Steadfast no more: *Iliad* 10.93–4.

74 *To Atticus, at Rome*   *Formia, March 26, 49 B.C.*

Dated March 26: rather, Cicero received the letter on that day.

'Resources' ... 'support': The distinction in Latin is between the plural *opes* and the singular *opem*.

p.119   **The moderation he showed at Popoli**: This is Corfinium, where Caesar forced Domitius to surrender, and then offered the garrison the alternative of joining his army or departing in safety.

That I should be true to my character and they to theirs: This combination of superiority and arrogance aroused hatred even among those whom he 'pardoned', and eventually led to his death.

75 *To Atticus, at Rome*   *Formia, March 28, 49 B.C.*

Cicero has had an actual interview with Caesar.

Your going to Spain or transferring forces to Greece: These are the two immediate tasks in front of Caesar, and in this order; he must deal with the legions under Afranius and Petreius in Spain first, and then follow Pompey to Greece.

p.120   **His house at Pedum**: near Rome.

A letter from Cicero to Caesar (*Ad Att.* IX 11A), in which he hoped to influence him towards peace by soft language and compliments, has been circulated at Rome. Cicero is embarrassed, but justifies himself by quoting a letter from Pompey to Caesar of an earlier date, with the same aim.

My approval of his case: What Cicero wrote in the letter was, 'I judged that you were the injured party in the war, in that your enemies and those envious of you were opposing an honour given to you by the Roman people', which is certainly some way from what Cicero saw as the true situation.

Pompey himself exhibited in public that letter: The letter in question was sent in reply to an approach from Caesar at the beginning of the war; it is referred to at *Ad Att.* VII 17.2.

His own and Scipio's: Pompey's career had been consistently brilliant; the Scipio referred to is Aemilianus.

Sextus Peducaeus: a close friend of Atticus.

77 *To Atticus, at Rome*   *Arpino, April 1, 49 B.C.*

p.121   **Men are being called up**: by the Caesarians now.

78 *To Cicero, at Formia,*
from Caelius   *Near Marseilles, April 16, 49 B.C.*

Caelius is at Marseilles, on the way to Spain with Caesar's army.

p.122   **In a rage with the senate**: Caesar had tried to restore the appearance of constitutional government in Rome. This led to tribunes, particularly L. Metellus (**73**), attempting to use their veto.

The cause on whose victory our own welfare depends: Caelius and others were deeply in debt, and had joined Caesar at least partly in the hope that his victory would lead to a cancellation of debts.

When Caesar arrives: i.e. Caesar's arrival in Spain will lead to immediate capitulation.

79 *To Atticus, at Rome   Cuma, near Naples, May 19, 49 B.C.*

p.123   **Hortensius**: son of the orator. He has been put in charge of the coast, and seems to be keeping a watch on Cicero.

81 *To Atticus, at Rome   Brindisi, November 27, 48 B.C.*

p.126   **The outlawing of individuals**: Cicero is speaking of proscription, for which Sulla's return in 82 provided the precedent.

'You': Atticus kept on good terms with everybody, including Antony. This is of benefit to Cicero, because he thus has the chance of making respresentations to those in power; but it would not have made Atticus popular if the Pompeians had won.

The bodyguard given me by the people: These are his lictors (see n. 1 below). It is ridiculous of Cicero still to be hoping for a triumph for his petty successes in 51. He kept the lictors until after his interview with Caesar in late 47, and then dismissed them.

Oppius and Balbus: agents and friends of Caesar.

Trebonius: C. Trebonius, Caesarian, praetor this year, consul in 45.

Pansa: C. Vibius Pansa, leading Caesarian, perhaps praetor this year; consul with Hirtius in 43.

p.127   **He was an honest, clean and upright man**: These are the Roman virtues; the Latin words are *integer*, *castus*, *gravis*.

82 *To Atticus, at Rome   Brindisi, June 19, 47 B.C.*

Caesar's having left Alexandria: He went there after Pharsalus in 48, and stayed for nine months. At one point he was in considerable danger from the city mob.

Antony: in control of Italy, as Master of the Horse to the Dictator Caesar.

Whether there is fighting in Italy or Caesar decides to use his fleet: This refers to the surviving Pompeians, now regrouped in North Africa. It was expected that they might invade Italy; alternatively, Caesar might transport his own army across to Africa, as in practice he did.

83 *To Atticus, at Rome* *Brindisi, July 5, 47 B.C.*

My poor daughter: Tullia is in poor health, and estranged from her husband Dolabella.

The crisis is coming now: Cicero was convinced that the Pompeians in North Africa and Spain were a real threat to Caesar's side. If they should win, his own position (as he had not joined them) would be perilous. In any case, he expects confiscations in Italy, whether from them or from the Caesarians; and so wishes Atticus to realise what capital he can.

The present regime will collapse: There have been disagreements among the Caesarians in Italy, particularly between Antony and Dolabella (now a tribune).

84 *To Atticus, at Rome* *Brindisi, July 9, 47 B.C.*

p.128 **My poor girl**: Tullia.

The will: Cicero speaks of Terentia's will in a number of letters around this time (cf. **85**). The details are unknown, but he is evidently worried about possible confiscations of his own and his wife's property, and wishes to provide for Tullia if it is humanly possible.

Nocturnal raids on houses: the irregular behaviour of wild young men in Rome.

Metella: SB deduces (*Ad Att.* Vol. V, p. 412) that this was the wife of P. Lentulus Spinther (son of the consul of 57), daughter of Metellus Celer (consul 60) and the notorious Clodia.

His statue of Clodius: If the text is correct, as seems very probable, Dolabella had demonstrated his radical views as tribune by setting up a statue to Cicero's old enemy.

85 *To Atticus, at Rome*   *Brindisi, August 6, 47 B.C.*

p.129   **Twelve sestertia**: 12,000 sesterces; not a large sum of money.

86 *To Terentia, at Rome*   *Venosa, October 1, 47 B.C.*

This is the last letter to Terentia in the collection. It and other short letters to her about this time seem formal and cool. The divorce followed.

Summary on p. 129

In three years he produced the series of discourses and dialogues: The amazing list is as follows (works no longer surviving are bracketed):

46 B.C. (The pamphlet *In praise of Cato*) and a number of rhetorical treaties: *Brutus*, *Orator*, and minor works.

45 B.C. After the death of his beloved daughter Tullia came the full flow of philosophical writings: (*Consolatio*), (*Hortensius*), *Academica* in four books, *De Finibus* in five books.

44 B.C. *Tusculan Disputations* in five books, Translations of Plato's (*Protagoras*) and *Timaeus*, *De Natura Deorum* in three books, *De Divinatione*, *De Fato*, *De Senectute*, *De Amicitia*, (*De Gloria* in two books), *De Officiis* in three books.

87 *To Varro*   *Rome, early in 46 B.C.*

Some of the work of M. Terentius Varro, voluminous writer and antiquarian, survives. Cicero always gives the impression of being in awe of him; letters like this one are formal and self-conscious.

88 *To Atticus*   *Rome, April, 46 B.C.*

p.130   **Murcus**: L. Statius Murcus, an officer in Caesar's army, became praetor in 45. This rumour is incorrect.

Pollio: famous now and in the future. See Letter **145** and n. 1 on p. 187.

The Balearics: the islands of Majorca and Minorca, off Spain.

Paciaecus: a Spaniard like Balbus, a follower of Caesar.

p.131   **Je m'en fiche**: 'I don't care'. (Wilkinson chooses a French expression to represent a Greek one in Cicero's letter.)

Pleasure, not duty: Here and in the following letters, Cicero recurs to the basic differences between Stoic and Epicurean philosophy. Atticus is an Epicurean, which explains the phrase 'you slumber on'.

Now is the time to solve the problem: He means that he and Atticus must make a careful assessment of what to do in present circumstances.

89 *To Varro, at Tusculum*   *Rome, late in April, 46 B.C.*

This feverish rejoicing: The Civil War seems to be over, and Rome is full of the victorious Caesarians.

p.132   **Baiae**: a luxurious holiday resort on the bay of Naples.

To compose Republics: as Plato, and Cicero himself (cf. **27**).

My red-letter day: because they will meet after all.

About Cato: Cicero was encouraged by Brutus to write a eulogy of Cato, who had committed suicide after the battle of Thapsus in Africa. He did so, as did Brutus himself and others. Caesar was sufficiently irritated by this to publish two pamphlets himself called 'Anti-Cato's (**106**). Sadly, Cicero's work has not survived, apart from two sentences quoted by later writers.

It would take an Archimedes: rather, 'it is a problem as difficult as those posed by Archimedes'. Archimedes, the greatest mathematician of the ancient world, sometimes amused himself by publishing problems for others to solve.

Aledius: not identified.

91 *To Paetus, at Naples*   *Tusculum, near Rome,*
early in July, 46 B.C.

L. Papirius Paetus, recipient of a block of letters in the ninth book of *Ad Fam.* (IX 15–26), was a rich Epicurean living in Naples. Five of the letters are quoted in succession here.

p.133   **Silius**: probably P. Silius, a contemporary and friend of Cicero's, often mentioned in the Letters.

Previously I thought that it was my business to speak freely: Cicero is referring to the early 50's, when he tried to speak out, mindful of his defence of the state against Catiline.

My reputation as a wit: Cicero was famous for his witty sayings, often personal in kind, which may have added to the hostility of such as Clodius (**6**) and Hirrus (**43**).

p.134   **Your brother Servius**: or cousin. This was Servius Clodius, an important figure in the beginnings of scholarship at Rome (Suetonius, *On Grammarians*, 3). When he died in 60, Paetus had given his library to Cicero.

Caesar having now filled whole albums: Caesar is known

to have made a collection of witticisms (Suetonius, *Life of Julius*, 56).

The *Oenomaus* of Accius: Accius was the last of the early Roman tragic writers, living 170 to 86 B.C. His plays are lost, but Cicero quotes from them frequently. (Oenomaus was the king of Elis whose daughter Hippodameia Pelops married after the famous chariot race.) The quotation from Accius' play apparently said that the stout and constant heart was firm as a rock against the attacks of envy (see below).

The only philosophers: i.e. the Stoics.

I perceived the ideal solution: Cicero does not claim this. What he says is, 'I had the right attitude to what was happening.'

How the greatest sages behaved under tyranny: He is thinking of Socrates under the Thirty Tyrants (404) and Plato at the court of Dionysius II at Syracuse in 366.

Not a comedy but a farce: The Latin words are 'Atellan' and 'mime'. Atellan farce was old Italian native comedy (cf. **23**); mime was the low popular entertainment at Rome.

p.135 **Hirtius and Dolabella**: Cicero was teaching the art of public speaking to these Caesarians, who had learned their politics in the army. Dolabella seems to be close enough, in spite of the trouble about the divorce and the dowry (**84**).

Phamea's dinner: Phamea was an acquaintance rather than a friend of Cicero's (*Ad Att.* XIII 49).

Selicius' house: Presumably Cicero had been thinking of buying it.

92 *To Paetus, at Naples*   *Tusculum, near Rome,*
                                             late in July, 46 B.C.

My pupils: Hirtius and Dolabella; see above.

p.136 **King Dionysius**: the tyrant visited by Plato (**91**). He was driven out of Syracuse in 344.

In bed: Cicero was ill when Pharsalus was fought (cf. p. 125).

Your friend Lentulus: i.e. Lentulus Crus, consul of 49, murdered like Pompey in Egypt.

Scipio, Afranius: ex-consuls; both died in Africa.
To do likewise when I choose: to commit suicide.
By selling your valuation-lands: See p. 135 and n. 2.

93 *To Paetus, at Naples*   *Rome, August, 46 B.C.*

p.137   **Not that you ever had more estates**: p. 135 and n. 2.
Verrius: also mentioned in **94**.
Camillus: a business man in Rome.

94 *To Paetus, at Naples*   *Rome, Autumn, 46 B.C.*

p.138   **Volumnius Eutrapelus**: a man-about-town in Rome. There
are two letters from Cicero to him in the collection.
    A course with a philosopher: the Epicurean Dion; see
below.
    The pattern and cynosure: The quotation comes from
Roman tragedy, probably Ennius or Accius.
    Aristippus: founder of the Cyrenaic school of philosophy,
more hedonistic even than the Epicureans. Lais was a
famous Corinthian *hetaira* (courtesan).
    It's better in the Greek: which is lit., 'I possess Lais, but
am not possessed.'
    The austerity law: Julius Caesar passed a sumptuary law
in this year (46), restricting extravagance.

95 *To Paetus, at Naples*   *Rome, Autumn, 46 B.C.*

p.139   **With my well-known heroism and philosophy**: This is a
bitter comment. All Cicero's philosophical teaching was that
there are more important things than life. See **96** and n. 1
on p. 140.

96 *To Cassius, at Brindisi*   *Rome, early in 45 B.C.*

This is to C. Cassius Longinus, the eventual tyrannicide.

p.140 **Yours is in the kitchen**: Cassius too is an Epicurean.

97 *To Cicero, from Servius Sulpicius*   *Athens, March, 45 B.C.*

This is one of the most famous letters in the correspondence, a letter of consolation composed by Cicero's old
friend Servius Sulpicius Rufus, consul of 51 and one of the
greatest of Roman jurists. There were conventions for the
genre of consolation, observable in the various examples we
possess. Sulpicius represents that 1) So much misery already
exists in the Roman world that this is a small addition;
2) What could Tullia have had to look forward to? 3) All
human life and achievement is transient; we are all born
mortal; 4) She had much happiness and satisfaction when
she was alive; 5) You have often consoled others; physician,
heal thyself! 6) Mourning becomes less intense in time; it is
up to the wise man to anticipate this process; 7) She would
not herself wish you to go on too long. The commonplace
nature of these arguments might seem to us formal and
laboured; but in the ancient world, among trained and
educated people, care taken and perfection of style were
tokens of affection and a tribute to friendship.

p.141 **Aegina, Megara, the Piraeus, Corinth**: Here, in the centre
of the letter, like a mythological example in a lyric poem by
Pindar or Horace, is a brilliantly conceived illustration of
the impermanence of human fortune. The Saronic gulf had
been the centre of commercial and political activity from the
earliest times in Greece. Aegina was a great trading nation,
a rival to Athens, until she was conquered by her in 459
B.C. and lost her independence for ever. Megara was
a small Dorian town on the borders of Attica, not big
enough to retain her freedom from her powerful neighbour. The Piraeus was the largest harbour in Greece,
where once there had been long walls stretching down
from the city of Athens to the sea, so that in the Pelopon-
nesian war Athens and Piraeus together were like an island;

but since the Macedonian take-over at the end of the fourth century Athens became a second-class city, of little political significance. Corinth, with her position at the isthmus ideal for trade on both land and sea, had been the wealthiest city in Greece ('wealthy Corinth' even to Homer); but she was comprehensively destroyed by the Romans in 146 B.C. Sulpicius has thought up a striking image.

98 *To Servius Sulpicius, in Greece*   *Ficulea, near Rome, April, 45 B.C.*

Cicero's reply.

p.143   **Quintus Fabius** (Maximus): the great general who fought Hannibal, commanding Roman armies for years during the Second Punic War, and consul five times. His son was consul in 213. Cicero refers in *De Senectute* (*On Old Age*) 12 to the speech Fabius made at the funeral of his son.

(Lucius) **Aemilius Paullus**: the general who defeated King Perseus of Macedon at the battle of Pydna in 168, who had four sons; but two were adopted (into the Fabian and Scipio families) and the other two died suddenly at the time of his triumph for his victory in Greece. The contrast of public joy and private sorrow is brought out by Livy (XLV 41).

(C.) **Sulpicius Gallus**: a contemporary of Aemilius Paullus, who also lost a young son.

Marcus (Porcius) **Cato**: the most distinguished and influential man at Rome in the early second century, the main speaker in Cicero's dialogue *On Old Age*, who lost his eldest son, then praetor designate, in 152, when Cato himself was over eighty years old. The self-control of the old man was much admired.

p.144   **One man**: Caesar, of course.

99 *To Atticus, at Rome*   *Astura, near Anzio, March 11, 45 B.C.*

The shrine to Tullia: This was not to be a normal tomb or memorial, but an actual temple, as to a god.

The essay I told you about: This was a work called *Consolatio*, addressed to himself. It has not survived.

Philippus: L. Marcius Philippus, consul 56, had a villa near Cicero's at Astura.

100 *To Atticus, at Rome   Astura, near Anzio, March 14, 45 B.C.*

Changes of ownership: The Romans were concerned, as Cicero is here, about the future care of tombs and memorials, when the land on which they were placed changed ownership.

101 *To Atticus, at Rome   Astura, near Anzio, March 16, 45 B.C.*

Terentia's dowry: to be repaid because of the divorce.

Arpino: Cicero's original home, in the centre of Italy, south of Rome.

102 *To Atticus, at Rome   Astura, near Anzio, March 28, 45 B.C.*

p.146 **Publilia**: Cicero's new wife; Publilius is her brother. The marriage did not last a year, under the strain of Tullia's death. Cicero was now sixty.

Young Marcus: now aged about twenty.

Bibulus: son of the consul of 59.

Acidinus: not known.

Messalla: M. Valerius Messalla Corvinus, son of the consul of 61, will become one of the most important men in Rome in the next generation, under Augustus; a great soldier, orator, and patron of a literary circle which will include Tibullus.

103 *To Julius Caesar, in Spain*   *Astura, near Anzio,*
late in March, 45 B.C.

The thirteenth book of Cicero's *Letters Ad Fam.* is com-
pletely composed of letters of introduction and recommendation to provincial governors and others, seventy-nine in all.
Such an exercise of personal influence (*gratia*) was an
essential part of Roman life. This is an unusual example.
What the great man (Caesar) and Cicero had in common
was a love of literature. The quotations here are all from
Greek authors, and constitute a kind of apologia for
Cicero's opposition in the past, together with an indication
that he was not plotting against Caesar now.

p.147   **When I was invited to do so by you**: The reference is to
Caesar's approaches to Cicero in 49 (cf. **66**), rather than his
invitations in 59 (cf. **9**).

     The quotations come from *Odyssey* 7.258, *Odyssey* 1.302
(= 3.200) + 24.315, *Iliad* 22.304−5, Euripides, fr. 905
(Nauck), *Iliad* 1.343 (and elsewhere), *Iliad* 6.208
(= 11.784).

105 *To Atticus, at Rome*   *Astura, near Anzio, May 3, 45 B.C.*

p.148   **I can't imagine anything ruder**: M. Junius Brutus was a
self-satisfied, inconsiderate man, whose moral standing in
Rome was nevertheless very high.

106 *To Atticus, near Rome*   *Astura, near Anzio, May 9, 45 B.C.*

p.149   **The brochure Hirtius has sent me**: Hirtius evidently gave
literary assistance to his leader (he wrote the Eighth Book
of Caesar's *Gallic War*), as well as being a most loyal
general. The brochure mentioned here is a collection of
material for Caesar to use in his Anti-Cato (cf. **90**).

     So I've sent it on to Musca: Cicero feels that the praise of
himself outweighs the denigration of Cato. Musca will have
been an agent of Atticus.

107 *To Atticus, at Rome*   *Tusculum, near Rome, May 26,*
                                                          45 B.C.

Faberius: Caesar's private secretary. Cicero had lent him money (**108**).

The letter to Caesar: This was an idea of Cicero's first mentioned in *Ad Att.* XII 40.2 on May 9 (in the continuation of Letter **106**). His plan was a letter of flattery and advice, like certain published letters to Alexander the Great by Aristotle and Theopompus, and indeed the surviving, but almost certainly spurious, *Letters* of Sallust to Caesar. Cicero had composed a draft of this letter, and sent it to Atticus to show to some Caesarians (Hirtius, Balbus, Oppius?) to see what they thought; they had not liked it. Presumably Atticus had suggested redrafting. Cicero eventually gave up the project.

That pupil of Aristotle: Alexander.

This lodger with Romulus: The hint about assassination mentioned in n. 1 comes in a letter of about ten days before this, *Ad Att.* XII 45.3.

108 *To Atticus, at Rome*   *Tusculum, near Rome, May 27,*
                                                          45 B.C.

p.150 **The gardens . . . the house**: SB (Appendix III in Vol. V of the *Letters to Atticus*) clarifies the many references in the letters around this date to Cicero's hopes of buying a suitable property for the shrine to Tullia. The first choice is an estate which previously belonged to a man called Scapula, and is now in the possession of his four heirs, one of them called Otho. The location is Rome, across the Tiber from the Campus Martius, in the Campus Vaticanus.

Faberius: 107.

We must fall back on Clodia: This is the second choice, gardens belonging to one of the women called Clodia, probably one of the sisters of P. Clodius. SB attractively suggests that this was the notorious Clodia (Catullus' Lesbia), whose gardens on the Tiber, used for immoral purposes, are mentioned in Cicero's *Pro Caelio* 36.

Dolabella's debt: the repayment of Tullia's dowry.

My dear little Attica: Atticus' daughter, often mentioned in the *Letters*. She was now seven years old; and suffered from recurrent ill health.

My speech for Ligarius: given in 46, a fine appeal to Caesar for the 'pardon' of Q. Ligarius, a republican. Atticus acted as Cicero's publisher as well as his financial adviser.

Varro: Atticus was always recommending that Cicero should give M. Terentius Varro, the great scholar (see **87**, **89**), a part in one of his dialogues.

p.151 **Full measure**: Hesiod, *Works and Days*, 350.

On Aims: i.e. the *De Finibus*. It is indeed dedicated to Brutus.

The *Academica*: This was rewritten, changed from two books to four, and so as to include Varro (**110**). What has survived of this work is curious, namely the second book of the first version (called the *Lucullus*) and much of the first book of the second. The interlocutors in the latter are Varro, Atticus and Cicero himself. The subject of the dialogue is Theory of Knowledge; Cicero propounds the 'scepticism' of the Middle Academy.

Antiochus: See **111**.

Catulus and Lucullus: For Catulus, see **14**; L. Licinius Lucullus was the successful general against Mithridates up to 67 B.C.

Scapula: See on **108**.

p.152 **For Dolabella**: Cicero's relations with him continued friendly, in spite of Tullia's divorce and death.

I fear the Trojans' reproach: a favourite quotation of Cicero (cf. **60**). Hector's sensitivity to public opinion (*Iliad* 6.442 = 22.105) was his reason for fighting and dying.

111 *To Varro*   *Tusculum, near Rome, July 11, 45 B.C.*

What you promised: See **109**.

I am sending you herewith: rather, 'I am sending you'. In fact, on July 20 (Letter **112**) he still does not know for certain that Atticus has sent the books to Varro.

A quartette: the new version of the *Academica* (**109**).

The younger Academy: i.e. the New Academy, third stage of the development of the school founded by Plato.

Antiochus: Antiochus of Ascalon was head of the New Academy, successor to Philo (cf. **32**). Cicero had himself studied under Antiochus at Athens in 78—77.

112 *To Atticus, at Rome*   *Tusculum, near Rome, July 20,*
                                      45 B.C.

p.153   **The procession**: Caesar's statue was again (cf. **107**) carried in a procession at the beginning of Games in late July. It was carried next to a statue of victory.

Cotta's proposal: L. Aurelius Cotta, consul of 65, a relative of Caesar, whose mother was an Aurelia. What the proposal was on this occasion is not known, but may be guessed from the fact that at the beginning of the following year the rumour was rife in Rome that L. Cotta would propose that as the Sibylline books said that Parthia could only be conquered by a king, Caesar should take that title (Suetonius, *Life of Julius*, 79).

Something addressed to Caesar: See **107**.

113 *To Atticus, at Rome*   *Pozzuoli, December 21, 45 B.C.*

Julius Caesar had stayed one night at Cicero's villa at Pozzuoli. This letter is of course of fascinating interest. There are only three months till his assassination.

Philippus: consul of 56, married to Caesar's niece Atia, and thus step-father of the future Octavian.

Mamurra: Cf. **63**. What the news was is not stated; perhaps Mamurra's death.

He was taking a course of emetics: a practice recommended by medical practice of the time.

With food well cooked: from Lucilius, the early satirist.

He mounted and paraded the whole of his armed guard: presumably as a mark of honour, although many have wondered whether it was a precaution.

Nicias: Curtius Nicias of Cos, a grammarian, well known to Cicero, and to Dolabella (**118**).

114 *To Manius Curius, at Patras*   *Rome, January, 44 B.C.*

For Manius Curius, see Letter **61**.

Far from the madding crowd: a free translation (taken from Gray's *Elegy*). The literal meaning of Cicero's quotation (from a Roman tragedy, perhaps by Accius) is, 'where I shall hear neither the name nor the deeds of the house of Pelops'. Cicero is fond of this quotation (cf. **120**, **128**).

Whom the Caesarians declared to be consul: All actions by Caesar were doubtfully constitutional. He had held sole consulship for nine months of the year, and then had two consuls appointed.

Though he had performed the ceremonies, etc.: The election of quaestors took place at the *comitia tributa* (Assembly of Tribes), that of consuls at the *comitia centuriata* (Assembly of Centuries). Caesar simply switched. It was this disregard of constitutional niceties that so infuriated his opponents.

Caninius: C. Caninius Rebilus, a Caesarian general now rewarded for his loyalty.

Legal ownership . . . usufruct: the two claims to property under Roman law, absolute ownership and the right of possession.

Acilius: a Caesarian commander. Cicero's letter commending Curius to him is extant (*Ad Fam.* XIII 50).

115 *To Brutus and Cassius, on the Capitol*   *Rome, March 17,*
   from Decimus Brutus   *44 B.C.*

The first paragraph of this letter, written two days after the
assassination, is of extreme historical interest. Decimus
Brutus is governor of Cisalpine Gaul, having been praetor
in 45; Brutus and Cassius are praetors now. The conspirators are uncertain how to proceed after their earth-shaking
act. Antony has the immense advantage of the consulship.
Hirtius, a constitutional Caesarian, due to be consul next
year, seems to be trusted.

p.157   **Any of us**: i.e. any of the conspirators.
        A nominal mission: See n. 1 on p. 43.
        I am confident: a misprint; read: 'I am not confident.'

p.159   **We should be putting them in the wrong**: i.e. right-
thinking people would be appalled that the restorers of
liberty should need a bodyguard from the Caesarians.

116 *To Atticus, at Rome*   *c/o Gaius Matius, near Rome,*
                                             April 7, 44 B.C.

Gaius Matius was a personal friend of Caesar, author of the
impressive letter **138**.
     A rising in Gaul: The terminology is that of the ancient
fear at Rome, implying fighting in Italy itself. But in fact
Matius is referring to Transalpine Gaul and a possible revolt
of the tribes against whom Caesar had fought. See **118**
(end).
     Lepidus: See **145**.

p.160   **Brutus pleaded for Deiotarus at Nicaea**: Deiotarus was
king of Galatia in central Asia Minor. After Caesar had
defeated Pharnaces of Pontus at Zela in 47 ('I came, I saw,
I conquered'), he reorganised the local kingdoms, depriving
Deiotarus of some of his territory. Brutus' speech on his
behalf at Nicaea (see map on p. 158) would be when Caesar
was returning to Italy. Cicero himself defended Deiotarus at
Rome in 45 against a charge of having attempted to murder
Caesar.

At Sestius' request: perhaps to plead for the 'pardoning' of a Pompeian. For Sestius, see **2**.

118 *To Atticus, at Rome*　　　*Pozzuoli, near Naples, April 18, 44 B.C.*

p.161　**O Socrates and all the tribe of Socrates**: In other words, Cicero is grateful to his training in Greek philosophy, which has taught him to despise unimportant things.

Marcus Curtius: the friend about whom Cicero wrote to Caesar in 54 (Letters **24** and **25**). He was a committed Caesarian, so that it is not clear why he is 'arraigning us'; perhaps for having bungled?

Vetus: C. Antistius Vetus, in charge of Syria.

Caecilius: See p. 159 n. 2.

Volcacius: son of the consul of 66; now probably governor of Cilicia.

Let's leave that to Dolabella and Nicias: Dolabella is now consul, and will go to Syria as his proconsular province. For Nicias, see **113**.

Aurelius, put in charge by Hirtius: Hirtius was propraetor of Gaul in 45. This Aurelius has not been identified.

119 *To Atticus, at Rome*　*Cuma, near Naples, April 19, 44 B.C.*

Trebonius: C. Trebonius (cf. **81**) decoyed Antony just before the assassination of Caesar. He is proconsul, and has left for his province of Asia.

p.162　**'From land to land'**: probably from Aeschylus, *Prometheus Bound* 682.

120 *To Atticus, at Rome*   *Pozzuoli, near Naples, April 22,*
                                                          44 B.C.

   Fair was the deed: This may be a quotation from a lost
Greek source, or merely Cicero expressing himself in
Greek.
   The rights of Latins: an intermediate stage on the way to
full citizenship.

p.163   **Octavius**: This is the first mention of the future emperor,
adopted by Caesar in his will, and so (when the will is
treated as legally valid) to be called C. Julius Caesar
Octavianus.
   'Far from the madding crowd': 114.

121 *To Atticus, at Rome*   *Pozzuoli, near Naples, April 26,*
                                                          44 B.C.

   Sextus Clodius: SB has strongly argued that this man's
real name was Sextus Cloelius. He had been a supporter of
P. Clodius in the years around 56 B.C., when gang warfare
raged at Rome. He was exiled in 52 for the riots which
followed Clodius' death.

p.164   **I enclose a copy of my reply as well**: *Ad Att.* XIV 13B.
Antony's letter is included next in this selection, but not
Cicero's reply. The effusive warmth and friendship shown in
it are a little embarrassing for us to read.

122 *To Cicero, at Pozzuoli,*   *? Rome, April 24, 44 B.C.*
   from Mark Antony, Consul

   Young Publius Clodius: son of Cicero's enemy.
   Your fortunes are now beyond the reach of danger: an
ironical comment considering what is to come.

123 *To Atticus, at Rome   Pozzuoli, near Naples, May 2, 44 B.C.*

p.165   **Paetus' stockfish**: See **91**.

The cross or the precipice: See n. 1. Crucifixion was the death penalty of slaves; throwing off the Tarpeian rock (a sheer drop at the side of the Palatine hill) was a traditional punishment for many capital offences, including treason.

Leonides: also mentioned in **129**, **137**.

Xeno: commissioned to pay Marcus' allowance in Athens (cf. **102**).

125 *To Cicero, from Trebonius   Athens, May 25, 44 B.C.*

C. Trebonius was on his way to the province of Asia as proconsular governor (**119**).

p.166   **Cratippus**: an eminent Peripatetic philosopher greatly admired by Cicero. The Peripatetics were the school founded by Aristotle.

126 *To Mark Antony, Consul   Lanuvium, near Velletri,*
from Brutus and Cassius, Praetors   end of May, 44 B.C.

Another key document for the history of the time.

p.167   **Ex-servicemen**: Caesar's veterans.

The memorial to Caesar: p. 165, n. 1.

127 *To Atticus, at Rome   Tusculum, near Rome, June 2, 44 B.C.*

p.168   **The Eurotas**: the river of Sparta. See n. 2 below.

Persian Pavilion: rather Persian colonnade. This was another feature of Sparta (commemorating the battle of Plataea), imitated by Brutus in his villa.

Favonius: See **13**.

In so far as I don't think: What Cicero means is that in other circumstances he would certainly wish Brutus to go to Rome, and not to undertake a province either now or later; but as it is, he ought to go to Asia as arranged.

p.169   **Criticised Decimus Brutus**: It is not clear why. SB suggests that it was for not making better use of the troops at his command in Cisalpine Gaul.

'I never heard anyone . . .': She was going to finish, 'say that'.

Servilia promised: She was a powerful woman, and had influence with the Caesarians.

Prophet, what profit: a Greek quotation, from an un-identified comic poet.

Far from the madding crowd: See **114**.

Dolabella chose me: as a legate on his staff in the province of Syria to which he is going as proconsul with a five year command. The responsibilities of a legate were flexible.

p.170   **Leonides, Herodes**: Cf. **123**.

Statius: If the name is correct, it may be Quintus' freedman (**9**).

That shrine: the one for Tullia. The gardens of Scapula (see on **108**) had become less attractive when Cicero discovered that they were likely to be affected by some building plans of Caesar's (*Ad Att.* XIII 33a.1); and by now the whole plan for the shrine had been shelved. This is the last mention of it.

p.171   **Sextus Aelius, Manius Manilius, Marcus Brutus**: famous
legal authorities of the second century B.C.
   Scaevola: Q. Mucius Scaevola (pontifex, consul in 95,
Cicero's own teacher) codified Roman civil law in eighteen
books, from which Cicero has excerpted the relevant
chapter.

132   *To Atticus, at Rome   Pozzuoli, near Naples, July 9, 44 B.C.*

   Accius' *Tereus*: For Accius, see **91**. The *Tereus* would be
a tragedy on the mythological history of that king of Thrace.
Accius also wrote a *Brutus*, about Marxus Brutus' ancestor,
who drove out Tarquin the last king of Rome. Cicero's
suggestion that Brutus confused the two plays is a joke. The
occasion of the production was the festival mentioned in **128**
(p. 169 and n. 2).
   You know what I think of Greek shows: They are spoken
of derisorily in the famous letter to M. Marius (p. 62).
   My nephew Quintus: He was Atticus' nephew as well.
Cicero's brother Quintus and Pomponia were now divorced
and Quintus had married again (n. 1 on p. 172).
   You wouldn't believe how delighted I was: SB shows that
the terms used in this letter are affected by the fact that
young Quintus himself was to take it to Atticus. In another
letter (*Ad Att.* XVI 1.6) Cicero is more sceptical about the
reformation.

p.172   **Some writings**: probably the *De Officiis*, being composed
for the edification of young Marcus in Athens.
   Our sailing together: Cf. **119**, **130**. Cicero wishes to go
abroad for the rest of this year, while Antony is consul and
the situation in Rome is dangerous. Brutus is to go to Asia
Minor (**127**, **128**).
   Gnaeus Lucceius: a friend of Brutus.
   Venosa: in south Italy: see map on p. 29.
   They will not be there: The legions were coming from
Macedonia, and would cross to Brindisi (see on **140**).

Otranto: The Latin is Hydruntum; a harbour south of Brindisi, in the heel of Italy.

133 *To Atticus, at Rome   Pompeii, near Naples, July 17, 44 B.C.*

p.173   **We shall part company**: a bitter comment.
On Old Age: the work *De Senectute*, dedicated to Atticus.
It is the same essay: not (as might appear) *On Old Age*, but its successor, *On Glory* (cf. **134**).

134 *To Atticus, at Rome*   *Vibo Valentia, Toe of Italy,*
                                          July 25, 44 B.C.

I've been travelling: down the west coast of Italy.
Reggio: Rhegium, on the straits between Italy and Sicily. Patras is in Greece, Taranto along the coast of south Italy.
'Bound far across the seas': *Odyssey* 3.169.

p.174   **What profit hath thy journey now**: Cf. **128**.
On Glory: This work has not survived; nor has the Third Book of the *Academica*. It is interesting that Cicero should have kept a set of Introductions, ready for use at the beginning of his philosophical works. Their careful composition is evident from the surviving works.

135 *To Mark Antony, Consul,*   *Naples, August 4, 44 B.C.*
       from Brutus and Cassius

This is a strikingly hostile letter. The tyrannicides loathed and mistrusted Antony.
Your manifesto: There have been various public statements from the consul and these two praetors. The Latin term is *edictum*.
Requested something from a consul in a manifesto: It is thought that they had asked to be relieved of the corn commission (**127**).

p.175 **On how long he did not reign**: rather, 'how briefly he reigned'.

Compatible: add *with*.

136 *To Atticus, at Rome*   *At sea, off Pompeii, August 19,*
                                          44 B.C.

p.176 **A proclamation of Brutus and Cassius**: perhaps the one referred to in **135**.

On the 1st: August 1st, the same meeting as that mentioned in the next paragraph.

Your words: The phrase 'Our friend Brutus makes no comment' was quoted (from a letter of Atticus) a little earlier in this section of the letter, and was explained by, 'He does not like to give advice to an older man'; i.e. Brutus has his opinions but is too respectful of Cicero to voice them.

Piso: Caesoninus, Cicero's old enemy, consul of 58, against whom the vituperative speech *In Pisonem* was composed.

To see the Olympic Games: This seems a minor matter for criticism. Cicero's words may be ironical.

137 *To Tiro, from young Marcus Cicero*   *Athens, August,*
                                                       44 B.C.

An attractive letter from the young university student to the family retainer.

p.177 **The errors of my youth**: Marcus had been living a wild life in Athens, helped by the over-generous allowance from his father (**102**).

Cratippus: **125**.

Mitylene: on the island of Lesbos. Cratippus had recently moved from there to Athens.

Epicrates: apparently a leading citizen of Athens.

Leonides: **123**, **129**.

Gorgias: a young lecturer who had been leading Marcus

astray (according to Plutarch's *Life of Cicero*, 24.8). Later he lived in Rome as a rhetorician.

138 *To Cicero, from Gaius Matius* *Rome, end of August,*
44 B.C.

Another famous letter, from an honest man. For Matius, cf. **116**.

p.179 **That very law**: either the same or a similar one to that from which Paetus suffered (p. 135 and n. 2).

p.180 **The festival which the young Caesar gave**: Octavian made his mark with the people of Rome by giving Games which Caesar had promised, for his victory in the Civil War. They had been held at the end of July.

p.181 **In retirement at Rhodes**: The status of Rhodes as an allied city, together with its other advantages, made it a favoured haven for Romans living in exile.

139 *To Cassius, near Naples* *Rome, late in September, 44 B.C.*

Speech: the *First Philippic*, given in the senate on September 2. There are fourteen *Philippics* in all, between this time and April 21, 43.
Piso: **136**.
Publius Servilius: consul in 48.
The house that used to be Metellus': a villa at Tivoli, previously belonging to Metellus Scipio, consul in 52, and now appropriated by Antony.

p.182 **A den of vice and drunkenness**: Cicero frequently attacks Antony's private life in the *Philippics*.
Disgorging: The word used is 'vomiting'.

140 *To Atticus, at Rome*   *Pozzuoli, near Naples, November 2,*
44 B.C.

The political complications are extreme. Apart from the civilians in the senate, many of them republican sympathisers and ex-Pompeians, and the tyrannicides, now absent from Rome, and Sextus Pompeius, with an army of Pompeians in Spain, there are three separate groups among the Caesarians. They are:— the consul Antony, mistrusted and feared, but able and active; Hirtius and Pansa, the consuls elect, intending to behave constitutionally; and the young Octavian, an unknown force, thrown into the maelstrom at the age of eighteen, but with one great advantage over everyone else, the name of Caesar. He is ready now to risk confrontation with Antony.

The three legions from Macedonia: 132. Antony had originally been allocated the proconsular province of Macedonia. On June 3 a change was made, and he was given instead the proconsular command of Cisalpine and Transalpine Gaul for five years, but with permission to keep command of the legions in Macedonia. These are the three legions summoned to Italy; a fourth was following.

Along the Adriatic coast: They are marching north from Brindisi.

141 *To Atticus, at Rome*   *Pozzuoli, near Naples, November 5,*
44 B.C.

p.183   **Willing to wound**: from Pope. Cicero's quotation is from *Iliad* 7.93 and means rather, 'ashamed to refuse, but afraid to accept', of the Greek leaders challenged to single combat by Hector.

142 *To Trebonius,*   *Rome, February 2, 43 B.C.*
Governor of West Asia Minor

p.184   **I reviewed the whole situation**: This was the *Third Philippic*.

Servius Sulpicius: Cicero's old friend, consul in 51, who had written him the famous letter of consolation (**97**). He had been sent on an official embassy to Antony by the senate, and died in the course of it. Cicero's *Ninth Philippic* is a warm tribute to him.

Lucius Caesar: consul in 64. His sister Julia was Antony's mother.

p.185 **Detached two legions**: i.e. two of the three mentioned in **140**.

143 *To Brutus, at Durazzo*   *Rome, April 17, 43 B.C.*

The *Letters to Brutus* come at the end of the surviving correspondence, all dated between March and July 43. Their genuineness has long been questioned, but the result of much scholarly investigation has been to support the authenticity of all except I 16 and I 17 (Letter **146**).

I have been in no great haste: The text is uncertain, but more probably, 'I have been most energetic'.

My time of life: Plautus, *Trinummus* 319.

You'll be crushed: The word 'you' is in the plural; not Brutus alone, but the republicans.

145 *To Cicero, at Rome, from Pollio*   *Cordova, Spain,*
                                              June 8, 43 B.C.

For C. Asinius Pollio, see n. 1 below. This is an odd, excited letter. Pollio had served efficiently with Caesar, and had been sent to Spain to oppose Sextus Pompey and the last relics of the Pompeians. In the present difficult situation he seems to be holding aloof; after the coming together of the triumvirs at the end of this year he will join Antony.

p.187 **The younger Balbus**: See **71**.

Just like Caesar: There is a confused story in our sources (e.g. Suetonius, *Life of Julius*, 39) that Caesar once compelled a Roman Knight called Laberius, an author of mimes, to act in one of his own productions. This nullified his equestrian status, but Caesar restored it, behaving in the same way as Balbus to Herrennius Gallus here.

Borough Commissioner: The point of the title and of n. 2 below is that Balbus, being a Spaniard, held a magistracy in his own city as well as the office of quaestor under Pollio.

Sextus Varus: A Sextus Quintilius Varus was praetor in 57. The words here indicate that he then went as governor to Spain.

At a gladiatorial show: The vicious cruelty of some Roman provincial governors is exceeded by this Spaniard.

p.188   **Lepidus**: M. Aemilius Lepidus, consul in 46, Master of the Horse to the Dictator Caesar in 46 to 44, and about to become the third member of the Second Triumvirate.

Cornelius Gallus: precursor of Propertius and Tibullus, perhaps founder of Roman love elegy.

146 *To Atticus, at Rome,*   *Macedonia, middle of June, 43 B.C.*
from Brutus

This is one of the two letters in the books *Ad Brutum* (I 16 and I 17) which are still suspected of being rhetorical forgeries of a later period. Brutus writes to Atticus about Cicero, in an uncompromising, unfriendly way. He thinks (probably rightly, however) that Cicero has made a serious mistake in putting his trust in Octavian. Even if it is a forgery, the author would be working from a close knowledge of the circumstances and personalities involved.

p.189   **He does not refrain from abusive remarks**: This alleges that Cicero, in trying to win Octavian to the cause, has gone so far as to criticise publicly the killing of Caesar, and to blame the leading tyrannicide Casca.

He put more than one person to death: The reference is to the execution of the Catilinarian conspirators in 63.

Bestia: tribune in 63, who attacked Cicero's treatment of the Catilinarians.

Proposes to give a new master a Triumph: to be more accurate, an Ovation; cf. **147** (end).

p.190 **Philippus**: Cf. **113**, **120**.

Even though Octavius may be a good man: The manuscripts have *Antonius*, but the reference must be to
Octavian.

My Portia's health: more correctly, Porcia, daughter of
Cato. She died soon after this.

What you asked: We have no means of telling what this
refers to.

147 *To Brutus, in Macedonia*   *Rome, middle of July, 43 B.C.*

p.191 **Your omission**: the failure to kill Antony as well as
Caesar.

A Brutus-like plan: referring, as often, to Brutus' ancestor
L. Junius Brutus who drove out the tyrant Tarquin, as well
as to the act of Brutus himself.

p.192 **The status of military commander**: A man could only
command a Roman army if he had the power (Latin:
imperium) granted to him by the senate or people. Cicero
had proposed that Octavian, too young to hold any office,
should be designated *propraetor*; this was in the *Fifth
Philippic*, delivered on January 1.

Philippus, Servius (Sulpicius), **Servilius**: consuls of 56,
51, 48.

The name of Brutus: Decimus, of course.

Larentia: A festival called the Larentalia was held on
December 23 each year.

Velabrum: a district in Rome, between the Tiber and the
forum.

Aquila: Pontius Aquila, one of the tyrannicides, had been
a legate of Decimus Brutus, and died, like the consuls, in
the battles at Modena.

Appendix

Cicero died on 7 December, 43. His brother Quintus and the younger Quintus also perished in the proscription. Cicero's son Marcus survived, to fight under Brutus at Philippi, and even to gain a consulship under Octavian in 30.

Others named in the *Letters* suffered the following fates:

L. Antonius (brother of Mark Antony): consul in 41; defeated by Octavian at Perugia in 40; died probably as governor of Spain not long afterwards.

Mark Antony: defeated by Octavian at Actium in 31; committed suicide in Egypt.

Attica (Atticus' daughter): married Octavian's friend and supporter Agrippa in 37; their daughter Agrippina was the first wife of the emperor Tiberius.

Atticus: lived on, a friend of both Octavian and Antony; died in 32.

Balbus: supported Octavian, as he had Caesar; achieved the consulship in 40.

Decimus Brutus: deserted by his troops when the triumvirate took over; was caught by Mark Antony and put to death, 43.

Marcus Brutus: committed suicide after the battle of Philippi in 42.

C. Cassius: took over the province of Syria, defeated Dolabella, and built up a formidable army; committed suicide during the battle of Philippi in 42.

Dolabella: defeated by Cassius in Syria; committed suicide, 43.

M. Favonius: fought on the republican side at Philippi; put to death after the battle.

Lepidus: played a progressively diminishing role as one of the triumvirs, until he was eased out totally in 36; he lived on until 12 BC.

Octavian: took over the Roman world after the defeat of Antony at Actium in 31; received the title Augustus in 27; died in 14 A.D.

Pollio: consul in 40; withdrew from political life before Actium; orator and literary figure; died in 4 A.D.

Tiro: died in 4 B.C. (at the age of ninety-nine according to Jerome, but this is now doubted).

Trebonius: captured and put to death by Dolabella in 43.

Varro: escaped the proscription; continued to write, the grand old man of Roman letters, until his death in 27 B.C. at the age of ninety.